# TOTALLY RANDOM QUESTIONS

## QUESTIONS

### VOLUME 6

# 101 Fascinating and Factual Q&As

Melina Gerosa Bellows

BRIGHT
MATTER
BOOKS

# Contents

# Lightning
## never strikes
## in the same place
# twice.

**#1**

**NOW YOU KNOW!**
Lightning strikes the Empire State Building roughly 25 times a year. It's protected by a special rod on the roof, which gives the lightning a safe place to strike.

ANSWER: **False**

**THE IDEA THAT LIGHTNING NEVER STRIKES THE SAME PLACE TWICE IS A MYTH.** Lighting usually strikes tall metallic objects, and **there is no reason why it couldn't strike the same tall metallic structure twice—or more.** Lightning is very hot and can heat the air around it to temperatures five times hotter than the sun. **The heat generated by lightning causes the air around it to vibrate, which creates the sound of thunder.** In areas that get a lot of lightning storms, preventative measures are taken to ensure houses and buildings are not struck. **Many houses have rods attached to the roofs** that conduct the lightning away from the house, keeping the structure and people inside safe.

**#2**

True or False:

Foxes don't **scream.**

*Ahhh!*

**THOUGH FOXES CAN MAKE ABOUT A DOZEN DIFFERENT SOUNDS** to communicate with other foxes, including barks and squeaks, their scream is the most bizarre. Unlike humans, **foxes usually do not scream because they're scared.** The screams usually come from vixens, or female foxes, **to attract male foxes.** The male foxes usually respond with a doglike *hup-hup-hup*. Another reason foxes scream is to **warn off predators** or other foxes that have gotten too close to their turf.

*Arctic fox*

**NOW YOU KNOW!**
Red foxes have such good hearing that they can hear rodents digging underground.

**Instant Genius**
Foxes can be found across the United States, from Alaska to Florida.

# The human body has enough iron to make a metal nail.

**#3**

*Hemoglobin molecule*

ANSWER: **True**

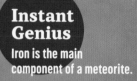

A 3-INCH (7.6 CM) NAIL CONTAINS 0.1 OUNCE (2.8 G) OF IRON, and the human body contains 0.1 to 0.14 ounce (2.8 to 4 g) of iron! What do we do with it? **Iron is essential to the body's ability to make a special protein called hemoglobin.** The protein, found in red blood cells, moves oxygen through your body. Oxygen allows your body to function and grow. Many people naturally produce enough iron. **If they don't, the condition is called anemia.** People who have anemia may feel tired and weak because their muscles are not getting the oxygen they need. **Eating iron-rich foods can help,** like seafoods, meats, beans, and peas.

# What is the
# largest
# planet
## in our solar system?

a. Earth

b. Venus

c. Jupiter

**Instant Genius**

Jupiter has an ocean of liquid hydrogen.

**ANSWER: C** **Jupiter**

**JUPITER IS THE LARGEST PLANET IN THE SOLAR SYSTEM** and about twice as large as all the other planets combined. **Jupiter is 11 times the size of Earth** and has 317 times its mass. This giant planet is fifth in line from the sun. Because Jupiter is the largest of the planets, its name is equally grand, as **Jupiter was the king of ancient Roman gods.** Jupiter is so far from the sun that it takes the planet the equivalent of 12 Earth years to make one lap around it. **Jupiter has rings,** but they are very faint and made mostly of dust.

**True or False:**

Cell phones carry 10 times more **bacteria** than a toilet seat.

#5

**WHEN WAS THE LAST TIME YOU SAW SOMEONE CLEAN THEIR PHONE?** Most people don't bother to do this very often, if at all. Now, **imagine all the places you put your phone** and all the people who have ever held it—it's probably picked up a lot of bacteria along the way! However, public restrooms are not the dirty places we often think they are. **Public bathrooms are usually cleaned daily,** so germs only live on surfaces for short amounts of time, and there is not a lot of lingering bacteria day to day. Next time you clean your room, **you might want to wipe off your phone too!**

### NOW YOU KNOW!
According to one study, the average person touches their phone 2,617 times a day.

### Instant Genius
Scientists have discovered a way to charge cell phones with urine.

# Where is the
# tallest
# mountain
## on Earth?

**#6**

**a. Hawaii**

**b. Nepal**

**c. Pakistan**

Duck, duck, nene.

**THOUGH MANY PEOPLE THINK THE TALLEST MOUNTAIN ON EARTH IS MOUNT EVEREST IN NEPAL,** it's actually Mauna Kea in Hawaii. Mount Everest has the highest altitude at a towering 29,032 feet (8,849 m), making it the tallest mountain above sea level. Although Mauna Kea only has a height of 13,796 (4,205 m) *above* sea level, it has another 19,700 feet (6,000 m) below sea level, bringing the mountain's total height to 33,496 feet (10,210 m). **That's 4,455 feet (1,358 m) taller than Mount Everest.** Mauna Kea is a volcanic island, which means it formed from a volcano erupting and producing rock over time. Because of its high peak, **Mauna Kea is home to the world's largest astronomical observatory.** Twelve scientific organizations from around the world have telescopes at Mauna Kea scoping out the sky.

**Instant Genius**

The state bird of Hawaii is the nene, also known as the Hawaiian goose.

**#7**

True or False:

Bats are
blind.

Gray long-eared bat

ANSWER: **False**

**BATS *CAN* SEE, AND MOST OF THESE MAMMALS HAVE DECENT EYESIGHT.** Some larger bat species called megabats can even see better than humans! **However, many bats are color-blind.** Unlike birds, these nocturnal hunters don't search for bright colors to find food. Instead, **bats that eat fruit and flowers are guided by shapes and their sense of smell.** Other bats rely on different senses to hunt. Insect-eating bats have excellent hearing and hunt using echolocation. **They send out a series of high-pitched sound waves** that bounce off objects, including their prey. These signals tell the bats how far they'll have to fly to catch their meal.

**Instant Genius**

Bats are more closely related to whales than they are to mice or rats.

**NOW YOU KNOW!**

Bats are responsible for the pollination of more than 300 fruit species, including mangoes, bananas, and guavas.

What was the #8 **hottest** temperature ever recorded on Earth?

**a.** 105 °F (41 °C)

**b.** 115 °F (46 °C)

**c.** 134 °F (57 °C)

Death Valley

Mecca

**STOP**
Extreme Heat Danger
Walking after 10 AM not recommended

**ANSWER: C** **134 °F (57 °C)**

**THE HIGHEST TEMPERATURE RECORDED ON EARTH IS 134 °F (57 °C),** which was logged at Greenland Ranch **in Death Valley, California, U.S.A., on July 10, 1913.** Though that was the highest recorded temperature ever, the consistently hottest city on Earth is Mecca, Saudi Arabia, where the average temperature is 87.6 °F (30.9 °C). But in the summer, **keep your fans handy, because Mecca reaches up to 122 °F (50 °C)!** Because of climate change, extreme temperatures are on the rise all over the world. Cities are hard at work to **find new ways to protect people from the dangerous heat**. Students at Columbia University in New York City, for example, are creating a special film to put on roofs to reflect heat. In Paris, government officials are adding misters to their public transit stops so people can stay cool.

## Instant Genius

The coldest temperature ever recorded was –128.6 °F (–89.2 °C) at Vostok, Antarctica, on July 21, 1983.

## NOW YOU KNOW!

Snowflakes falling at 2 to 4 miles an hour (3 to 6 kmh) can take up to an hour to reach the ground.

# How long
## does it take a blood cell to make a
# complete lap
## around your body?

a. 1 minute

b. 45 seconds

c. 20 seconds

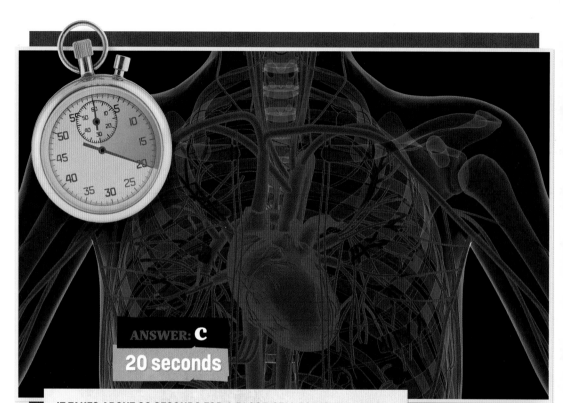

**ANSWER: C**

**20 seconds**

**IT TAKES ABOUT 20 SECONDS FOR A BLOOD CELL TO MOVE FROM THE HEART, THROUGH THE BODY, AND BACK TO THE HEART.** That's about how long it takes to sing the "Happy Birthday" song twice. **Starting in the heart, the cell gets pumped out to the lungs,** where it receives the oxygen it needs to deliver to the rest of the body. The heart then pumps the blood cell into the bloodstream, where it delivers oxygen to the muscles, kidneys, and other organs. **A single red blood cell can last about four months in the body.** Then your body makes new ones to replace them.

**Instant Genius**

An ounce (28 g) of blood has 150 billion red blood cells.

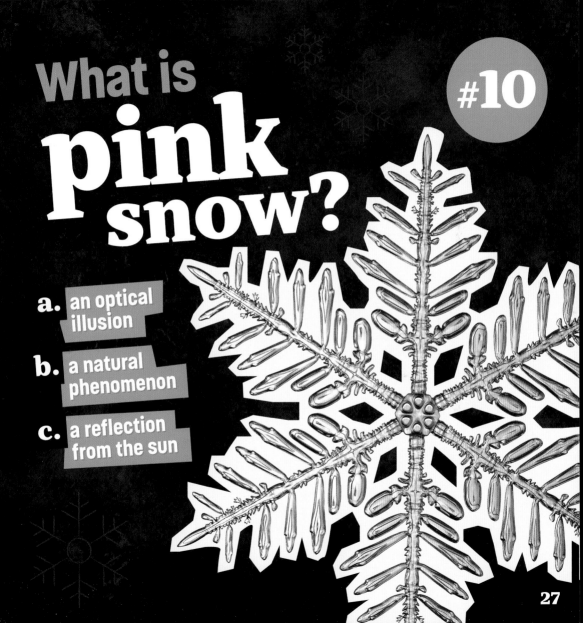

# What is pink snow?

a. an optical illusion

b. a natural phenomenon

c. a reflection from the sun

**a natural phenomenon**

**HOW IS SOME SNOW PINK? ALGAE!** Algae are neither animals nor plants, but little organisms that live all over the world. **There is one special alga species that turns the snow a red or pink color.** Unlike freshwater algae, this species thrives in freezing water. The algae are not naturally colored this way, but the chemicals they use to protect themselves from ultraviolet (UV) light are brightly colored. **Known as "watermelon snow,"** pink snow occurs in northern Italy and in the U.S. states of California and Colorado.

**NOW YOU KNOW!**
About 1 septillion snow crystals fall each year. That's 1,000,000,000, 000,000,000, 000,000!

**Instant Genius**

The largest snowflake ever recorded was 15 inches (38 cm) wide.

# They can use tools.

SEA OTTERS MOSTLY EAT HARD-SHELLED MARINE ANIMALS, including sea urchins, clams, mussels, and crabs. To break open tough shells, sea otters have a special trick. The clever critters dive down to a reef and collect rocks. Back at the surface, **they float on their backs, balancing their food on their bellies** as they use the rocks to break or pry open the hard shells. If a shell is extra tough to crack, **sea otters may make pit stops along the coast to bang their shelled meals against rocks.** These supersnackers are so good with their tools that they can eat up to 75 mussels in one hour.

**NOW YOU KNOW!**
Sea otters have the densest fur of any mammal. It's so thick that their skin never gets wet.

**Instant Genius**
Sea otters hold paws while sleeping so they don't float away from each other.

The length
of your
**foot**
is the same
as the length
of your
**forearm**
between
your wrist
and elbow.

**#12**

*Leonardo da Vinci self-portrait*

**SEE FOR YOURSELF! IF YOU PUT YOUR FOOT AGAINST YOUR FOREARM, YOU'LL SEE THEY ARE THE SAME LENGTH.** Leonardo da Vinci, an important thinker and artist from the 1400s, figured this out. **One of the many things he studied was the proportions of the human body.** To show what he learned, Leonardo drew a very famous picture of the human body called *Vitruvian Man*. This work of art details all the measurements of the human body, showing how the measurements compare. **The foot-to-forearm matchup isn't the only thing he discovered.** Leonardo also figured out that **a person's wingspan— the measurement from your left fingertips to right fingertips**—is the same as your height.

**NOW YOU KNOW!**
Leonardo da Vinci wrote from right to left, instead of left to right. He was also a vegetarian.

True or False:

# Passing gas can be dangerous for astronauts.

Gas flame

**ANSWER: True**

**PASSING GAS HAS THE POTENTIAL TO BE VERY DANGEROUS FOR ASTRONAUTS.** That's because the gases that humans, uh, excrete are **hydrogen and methane, both of which are very flammable.** Producing flammable gases in a small chamber in space means something could catch on fire or even explode. Because of this danger, **astronauts follow a special diet to help reduce their natural production of gas.** The diet consists of healthy foods such as grapefruit, almonds, fish, lettuce, and cottage cheese—all foods that produce **less gas than a diet high in carbohydrates like bread and pasta.**

What's the **#14** **deadliest** land mammal?

**a. lion**

**b. hippo**

**c. rhino**

## hippo

**THEY MAY LOOK CUTE, BUT HIPPOPOTAMUSES ARE THE DEADLIEST NONHUMAN LAND MAMMAL ON EARTH,** killing about 500 people in Africa every year. Hippos are herbivores, which means they mainly stick to eating grass and fallen fruit. Although hippos don't normally attack humans, **they can become aggressive toward people when they feel threatened.** They attack using very sharp canine **teeth that can reach up to 20 inches (51 cm) long,** and they can open their jaws almost 4 feet (1.2 m) wide! Weighing up to 4 tons (3,629 kg) with the ability to **run up to 30 miles an hour (48 kmh),** hippos—especially when aggravated—are very difficult to fight off.

**NOW YOU KNOW!**
The name "hippopotamus" comes from the Greek word for "river horse."

**Instant Genius**
The hippo's closest living relatives are whales.

#15

**True or False:**

Earth contains enough **gold** to cover the planet.

37

**ANSWER: True**

LONG AGO AS EARTH WAS FORMING, METEORITE SHOWERS OF GOLD AND MINERALS RAINED DOWN FROM THE SKY. The elements were so dense and heavy that they sank into Earth's core and stayed there. Over time, these meteorites deposited so much gold that **Earth's core now holds enough to cover the entire planet in 13 inches (33 cm) of the precious metal.** What stands between us and all that gold? **Earth is made of four layers:** the inner core (where the gold is located), the outer core, the mantle, and the crust. **The inner core is a solid metal ball at the very center of the planet.** The outer core surrounds it, followed by the thick mantle. Finally, the crust, the thinnest layer and the outermost surface of Earth, forms the ground we stand on.

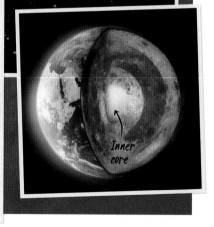

Inner core

How much does an average human skeleton weigh?

Where's my funny bone!

#16

a. about 25 pounds (11 kg)

b. about 50 pounds (23 kg)

c. about 100 pounds (45 kg)

## about 25 pounds (11 kg)

**OUR BONES MAKE UP 15 PERCENT OF OUR TOTAL WEIGHT.** So, if the average adult weighs around 165 pounds (75 kg), then their skeleton would weigh 25 pounds (11 kg). **The skeleton has a lot of jobs.** It supports your body weight and allows you to move around. Your skeleton also produces blood cells. **In the center of every bone is a substance called bone marrow,** which provides all the tools to build red and white blood cells. Each part of the skeleton also protects vital organs. The skull protects the brain, the rib cage protects the heart and lungs, and the backbone protects the spine. **The skeleton also stores minerals.** Bones hold calcium and vitamin D to keep you healthy and strong.

**NOW YOU KNOW!**

The longest bone in your body is the femur, which runs from your hip to your knee.

Bone marrow in the femur

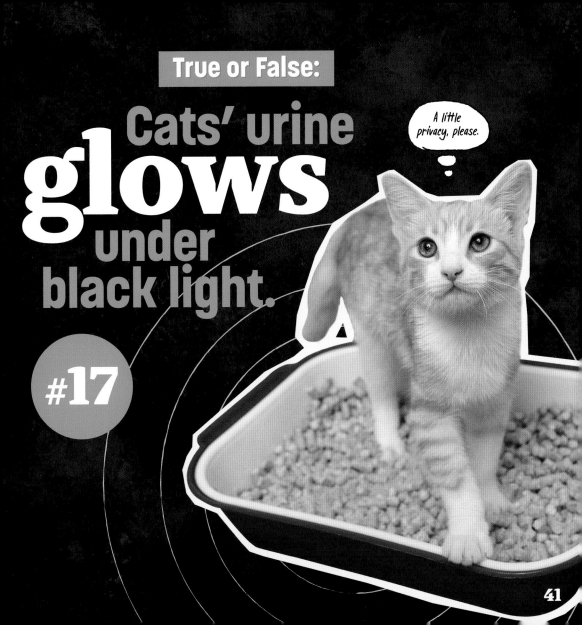

True or False:

Cats' urine glows under black light.

A little privacy, please.

#17

41

**ALL TYPES OF URINE—INCLUDING CAT, HUMAN, AND DOG—CAN BE DETECTED UNDER BLACK LIGHT.** That's because urine contains an element called **phosphorus, which naturally glows yellow or green with the presence of oxygen,** which is all around us. However, when the light is applied to cat urine, it *really* lights up. **People use black light to find where their cat might have, um, done its business in their home,** because the urine produces a strong ammonia-like odor when it reacts with bacteria. Apart from their pee, some animals themselves— including Tasmanian devils and wombats—glow a blue-green color under black light. **Scientists are trying to figure out exactly how and why this happens,** but phosphorus is unlikely to be involved.

*Hygiene is important!*

## Instant Genius

Male cat urine tends to smell worse than female cat urine.

**#18**

What is
the most
**sensitive finger**
on the
human hand?

**a.** the pinkie    **b.** the index    **c.** the thumb

**THE INDEX FINGER, FOUND BETWEEN THE THUMB AND MIDDLE FINGER, IS ALSO KNOWN AS THE POINTER.** It's shorter than some other digits but is still **the most sensitive and flexible of all.** It's also one of the most frequently used fingers for hand function and nonverbal communication. **The pointer contains two muscles, one that allows it to stretch out fully, and the other that contracts it.** Its most sensitive area is the fleshy tip, thanks to a nerve that runs through it. **The index finger easily touches the thumb, which allows for a strong grip.** This pinching action is vital for manual tasks that require small, complicated movements.

Handy!

### Instant Genius

Aye-ayes, a kind of primate that lives in Madagascar, have six digits on each hand.

**#19**

True or False:

Snakes **chew** their food.

A water snake eating a fish

ANSWER: **False**

## Instant Genius

Five species of snake can "fly."

**NOW YOU KNOW!**
Pythons have very small leg bones beneath muscles attached to their pelvis near the end of their bodies. They look like tiny bumps.

**ALMOST ALL SNAKES GULP DOWN THEIR FOOD WHOLE!** Most snakes will swallow their prey alive or kill it first, either with a venomous bite or a tight squeeze. **Snakes have special jawbones** that allow them to engulf prey two to three times the size of their head. Depending on the size of the prey, **snakes can take hours—even days—to completely swallow their meal.** Digestion takes a long time. **Between meals, most snakes take a long break** that can last from a few days to a few months.

leg bone

**#20**

# How many **sweat glands** does the human body have?

a. Hundreds

b. Thousands

c. Millions

Sweat glands under a microscope

ANSWER: **C**

## millions

**HUMANS HAVE ABOUT 4 MILLION SWEAT GLANDS THROUGHOUT THE BODY.** There are two major types of sweat gland. **The first kind, eccrine glands, are the main sweat producers.** They are located all over your body and are most numerous on the palms of your hands, soles of your feet, and your forehead—and, of course, in your armpits. **The other kind, called apocrine glands, are larger and located in the groin, breast, and—yep—armpit areas.** Apocrine glands are activated mostly by hormones. **Puberty and heightened emotions,** such as stress and fear, cause excessive sweating in those areas.

**Instant Genius**
When we feel happy, we produce chemicals that others can smell in our sweat.

**NOW YOU KNOW!**
Sweat by itself does not naturally produce a smell. The sweat mixing with bacteria on the skin is what creates body odor.

**True or False:** **Fire** **#21**
can naturally burn in
**space.**

49

**FIRE IS A CHEMICAL REACTION BETWEEN OXYGEN, HEAT, AND A FUEL SOURCE LIKE FIREWOOD OR GASOLINE.** Space has no oxygen, so fire can't exist. But inside spacecraft like the International Space Station (ISS), scientists are actually trying to start fires. **It's dangerous to create flames (even by passing gas!) on the ISS,** so astronauts carry out their experiments in special containers using artificial oxygen. Why? **They want to understand what materials can more easily catch fire inside spacecraft,** which methods of putting out fires in space are most effective, and how fire in space behaves differently on a flat surface versus a round surface. By learning from these experiments, **scientists hope to make life in space safer for astronauts** and to improve the tools they use.

**NOW YOU KNOW!**
On Earth, flames are teardrop-shaped because of Earth's gravity. In space, flames would be round, like a sphere.

*Candle flame in zero gravity*

**Instant Genius**
Some forest fires can be seen from outer space.

*A forest fire in Australia*

# #22 What was *Adalatherium?*

**a.** an ancient man-eating flower

**b.** a beastly badger that lived 66 million years ago

**c.** the British naval ship that discovered the *Titanic*

**ANSWER: b**

# a beastly badger that lived 66 million years ago

A SURPRISINGLY WELL-PRESERVED 66-MILLION-YEAR-OLD BADGER SKELETON in Madagascar baffled paleontologists for many reasons. This badger was strangely large for the time period. **Most mammals that lived in the Mesozoic period were about the size of a mouse, whereas this badger would have been the size of a house cat.** The *Adalatherium* also had more vertebrae, or backbones, than any known animal in the Mesozoic period, and had an oddly shaped snout and legs. **Why was this badger so bizarre? It's likely because it lived on an island.** Animals that live in isolated environments, such as islands, grow and adapt differently from animals on the mainland. Many species on Madagascar and other islands today look very different from other known animals.

*Madagascar tomato frog*

**#23**

**True or False:**

Rain has a
# smell.

**TECHNICALLY, WATER DOES NOT HAVE A SMELL.**
But there is a scent associated with rain. This smell happens when the weather becomes humid before a rainstorm. **Called petrichor, the smell is created by chemical reactions in an ecosystem.** When the air becomes heavy with humidity before a storm, certain bacteria react in the soil and leaves on the ground. **The bacteria break down the leaves and decomposing matter, which creates a chemical called geosmin.** The chemical has such a strong smell that, when rain starts to hit the ground, the scent wafts into the air.

**NOW YOU KNOW!**
Rain droplets are not actually shaped like a teardrop. They are more of a hamburger bun shape.

**Instant Genius**
It takes the average raindrop two minutes to hit the ground.

# What is the largest lizard in the world?

#24

a. the crocodile monitor

b. the Asian water monitor

c. the Komodo dragon

*Where's the beef?*

# the Komodo dragon

**KOMODO DRAGONS ARE THE LARGEST, HEAVIEST LIZARDS ON EARTH.** These Indonesian reptiles start life in an egg the size of a grapefruit and can **grow to 10 feet (3 m) long as an adult.** They usually weigh around 150 pounds (68 kg), though **the largest dragons have been recorded to weigh more than 360 pounds (163 kg)!** Komodo dragons are scavengers and eat almost any meat they can find. They have been known to eat Timor deer, water buffalo, and—*gulp*—even other Komodo dragons. **They leave behind virtually no trace of their meals, devouring intestines, hooves, and bones.** They can easily stretch their stomachs when eating and are able to consume 80 percent of their body weight in one sitting, which explains some of their more extreme recorded weights.

## Instant Genius

Komodo dragons can smell rotting flesh from up to 5 miles (8 km) away.

### NOW YOU KNOW!

Komodo dragons use their tongues to smell when they hunt. Once they locate their prey, these reptiles use their venomous bite or their razor-sharp teeth to kill.

# Why is it so hard to **swat** a housefly?

**a.** They can read our minds.

**b.** They move too fast for humans to see.

**c.** They see the world in slow motion.

# They see the world in slow motion.

**TIME PASSES VERY DIFFERENTLY FOR HUMANS AND FLIES.** How? A fly processes what it sees much faster than we can. How fast an insect or another animal can process this visual information is called a flicker fusion rate. **Species with higher rates than humans see the world in slow motion.** For typical houseflies, that means **movements appear four times slower to them than they do to us.** If they see a swatter, shoe, or rolled-up newspaper starting to come their way, this ability gives them plenty of time to process what they're seeing and **make a quick escape.**

## NOW YOU KNOW!

Like humans, fruit flies have a brain that is wired to see colors. One study shows fruit flies are more attracted to ultraviolet light than green light.

## Instant Genius

Most flies travel at a speed of 4.3 miles an hour (7 kmh).

How far does the average human **walk** in a **lifetime?**

#26

**a.** 1,000 miles (1,609 km)

**b.** the distance from New York to California

**c.** the distance around the world five times

**THE AVERAGE HUMAN TAKES ABOUT 7,500 STEPS PER DAY.** If you were to walk that much every day until you were 80 years old, you would have walked about 216,262,500 steps in your lifetime! A person's average stride, or length of a step, is 2.2 to 2.6 feet (0.7 to 0.8 m), so **walking 216,262,500 steps in your lifetime would translate to about 110,000 miles (177,028 km).** If you're walking straight on the equator, that's about the same as walking around Earth five times. Though the average number of steps taken per day is 7,500, **the Centers for Disease Control and Prevention recommend 10,000 steps per day to maintain a healthy lifestyle.** That's roughly equal to walking 5 miles (8 km) a day. What are the benefits? **Walking can help keep muscles strong, blood flowing well, and even improve your mood.**

X-rays of the right foot

**NOW YOU KNOW!**
Your feet have 25 percent of the bones in your body and 8,000 nerves.

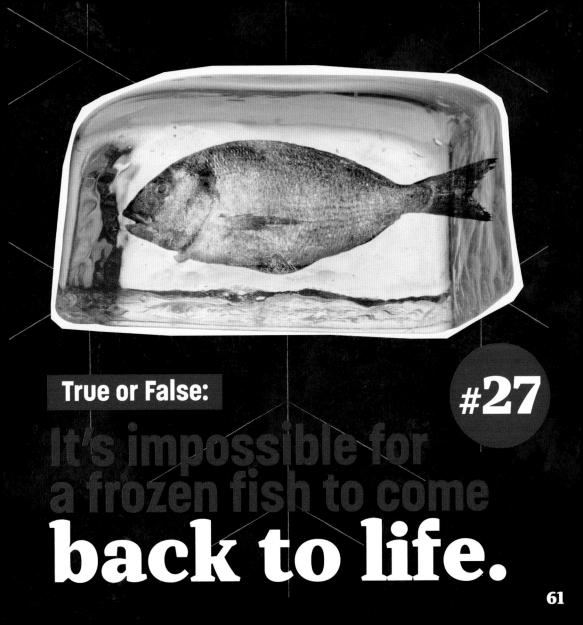

**True or False:**

**#27**

It's impossible for a frozen fish to come **back to life.**

Antarctic icefish

ANSWER: **False**

Weddell Sea, Antarctica

**AN ANTARCTIC ICEFISH, FROZEN IN A BLOCK OF ICE, CAN TOTALLY COME BACK TO LIFE!**
How's that possible? Fish are naturally cold-blooded, which helps them survive in extremely cold water. If seawater freezes, **fish that are used to cold water can produce special proteins that keep them alive.** These antifreeze proteins are in the fish's blood. **They attach to the ice crystallizing in the bloodstream and stop the fish's growth.** In icy waters, their metabolism can also slow down to a point where they are just barely alive, although they may look dead.

# What's special about Alaska's location?

**a.** It's the most eastern state in the United States.

**b.** It's the most western state in the United States.

**c.** It's both.

Welcome to
*Alaska*
and the Gateway to the Klondike

**It's both.**

**ALASKA IS BOTH THE UNITED STATES' MOST EASTERN AND WESTERN STATE.** How? Because parts of the state **cross the prime meridian, an imaginary vertical line that divides Earth into Eastern and Western Hemispheres,** just as the equator divides Earth horizontally into the Northern and Southern Hemispheres. Alaska, the 49th U.S. state, is important because of its location. **It is equally close to Asia and Europe,** and it can be reached by both sea and air travel. Because it can be more easily reached by other continents, Alaska is a strategic location for military bases. Alaska is also home to many natural resources and diverse wildlife. Plus, it's huge! **When Alaska joined the United States in 1959, it increased the size of the country by one-fifth.**

**Instant Genius**

In Alaska, there is one bear for every 21 people.

Mount Denali

**NOW YOU KNOW!**

Seventeen of the 20 highest U.S. mountains are located in Alaska. Mount Denali is the highest at 20,310 feet (6,194 m) above sea level.

# 29

# What do rabbits do when they're happy?

a. grunt

b. purr

c. stomp

Snuggle time, kittens.

**ANSWER: b**

purr

**RABBITS HAVE MANY SOUNDS AND ACTIONS THEY USE TO EXPRESS THEIR EMOTIONS.** Some of the most distinct sounds include grunts, thumps, and purring. **Though a rabbit purr may sound very similar to a cat's, rabbits do it differently.** Cats purr by opening and closing their vocal cords, and by using a special bone in their throat called the hyoid bone. Rabbits, however, make the sound by chattering their teeth together. Rabbits purr when they are happy or relaxed. **Another way a rabbit will express happiness is by jumping in the air and twisting its head or body back and forth.** This is called a "binky." A grunt means a rabbit either wants attention or is agitated, and **a thump of their back foot means a rabbit is upset.**

### Instant Genius

Baby rabbits are called kittens.

### NOW YOU KNOW!

Carrots are not part of a rabbit's natural diet. In the wild, rabbits eat lots of other plant matter, including grasses, flowers, and bark.

**True or False:** All owls have **symmetrical ears.**

#30

Hoo are you looking at?

Great horned owl

**NOW YOU KNOW!**
The barn owl swallows animals whole. After digestion, it coughs up the bones and skin.

ANSWER: **False**

**NOT ALL OWLS HAVE EARS YOU CAN SEE THROUGH THEIR FEATHERS**—but the great horned owl's asymmetrical ears are on full display. Why don't their ears line up? **Some owls have lopsided ears to better help the flying predators find prey on the ground below.** With one ear higher and the other lower, the owl hears sounds at two different times. **The different timing between the two sounds helps the owl zero in on its prey's location,** so it can swoop down with precision to grab its meal. **Owls have extremely sensitive hearing.** Some scientists think that it's so sharp that an owl could find its prey in complete darkness.

Barn owl eating a rat

# 31

# How much does the sun weigh compared to Earth?

**a.** They're about the same.

**b.** The sun weighs 3 times as much as Earth.

**c.** The sun weighs 333,000 times more than Earth.

# The sun weighs 333,000 times more than Earth.

**THE SUN WEIGHS ABOUT 333,000 TIMES AS MUCH AS EARTH.** How much is that exactly? Well, Earth weighs about 13 septillion pounds. That's a 13 with 21 zeros (about 6 septillion kg). In comparison, **the sun weighs about 4 nonillion pounds (about 2 nonillion kg). That's a 4 followed by 30 zeros!**

The sun is 864,400 miles (1,391,000 km) across, which is about 109 times the width of Earth. **The sun is so large that about 1,300,000 Earths can fit inside it!** It is also the central point of the solar system, with everything else revolving around it. The sun's gravity holds together the rest of the system, keeping everything from planets to dust in orbit. **Earth circles 93 million miles (150 million km) away from the sun.** Even at that distance, our planet's seasons, weather, and ocean currents are all directly affected by the sun.

## Instant Genius

If Earth were the size of a gumball, the sun would be as tall as the average front door of a house.

This illustration places Earth near the sun to show size difference between the two objects. Earth is not actually this close to the sun.

## NOW YOU KNOW!

The sun's core is about 27 million °F (15 million °C).

#32

If you hold in a **sneeze,** your eyes have a 10 percent chance of **popping out.**

**NEVER FEAR, HOLDING IN A SNEEZE WILL NEVER MAKE ENOUGH PRESSURE TO POP OUT YOUR EYES.** Still, it's better not to hold in a sneeze. **Though sneezing might feel weird, there is a good reason your body does it.** In your nose, you have lots of small hairs called cilia. When these hairs sense something they do not recognize, like dust or germs, **a signal is sent to the brain to initiate a sneeze.** The blast of the sneeze forces out the unknown substance from the nose, which helps keep the body safe from unwanted intruders like germs. **A sneeze can travel as far as 27 feet (8 m),** so grab a tissue to catch them when you can!

**NOW YOU KNOW!**
"Phantosmia" is the term for smelling something that isn't actually there.

**Instant Genius**
Smells and tastes can affect your mood.

# Which kind of animal traveled across the **Atlantic Ocean** millions of years ago?

**a.** a monkey

**b.** a horse

**c.** a snake

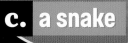

## a monkey

**SCIENTISTS HAVE DISCOVERED TOOTH FOSSILS FROM AN ANCIENT MONKEY IN THE SOUTH AMERICAN COUNTRY OF PERU** that trace back to an extinct group of African primates. This suggests that the monkeys traveled nearly 900 miles (1,448 km) across the Atlantic Ocean! Researchers estimate that this species made the journey roughly 34 million years ago. **During this time, Africa and South America were closer together and the sea levels were lower.** Monkeys aren't regular swimmers, so how did these primates journey all the way across the ocean? One theory: Because the sea levels were lower, **there may have been more islands that the monkeys could have crossed.** In areas with fewer islands, scientists think **the monkeys may have held on to floating trees that acted as sails,** making it possible for the monkeys to complete the journey.

**NOW YOU KNOW!**
The pygmy marmoset, the smallest monkey in the world, grows to just 4 to 5 inches (10 to 12.7 cm) long.

**Instant Genius**
Human DNA is more than 98 percent similar to the DNA of other primates.

# 34

# How was the diary of Anne Frank discovered?

**a.** Anne gave it to a friend.

**b.** It was found in an attic.

**c.** It was dropped on the street.

# It was found in an attic.

**ANNE FRANK WAS BORN IN GERMANY IN 1929.** When she was 10 years old, World War II broke out in Europe. **At that time, Germany was controlled by a political party called the Nazis, led by Adolf Hitler.** The Nazis hated Jewish people and wanted to kill them. **Being Jewish, Anne and her family were in great danger.** Her family moved from Germany to the Netherlands to escape the Nazis, but a few years later, the Nazis took control of that country, too. **On July 6, 1942, family friends helped the Franks go into hiding in an attic apartment in Amsterdam in the Netherlands.** For two years, Anne documented her life in hiding through her diary. On August 4, 1944, Anne and her family were discovered and taken by Nazi soldiers. **Unfortunately, Anne's father, Otto, was the only survivor.** Anne left her diary in the attic, where it was found by a family friend. **Anne's father published the diary in 1947,** and it would soon be taught in schools, helping people around the world to understand this terrible time in history.

What
is the
**oldest**
**sport**
in the
world?

#35

a. **wrestling**

b. **soccer**

c. **tennis**

**ANSWER: a** **wrestling**

**WRESTLING ORIGINATED 15,000 TO 20,000 YEARS AGO IN SOUTHERN EUROPE.** How do we know this? **Scientists found cave drawings depicting the sport in the Lascaux caves of France.** Wrestling was especially popular in ancient Egypt and Greece. In Greece, there were wrestling schools where young men would learn the sport, and events at the Olympic Games to showcase each man's abilities. **In ancient Egyptian tombs, archaeologists have discovered paintings and drawings clearly showing the many positions and techniques still used today.** But wrestling has been around a long time in other places, too. Around 5,000 years ago, the Sumerians of southern Mesopotamia (now western Asia) depicted wrestling on stone slabs, and an ancient bronze vase with wrestlers was also discovered in the Middle Eastern country of Iraq.

**Instant Genius**

Kite flying is a professional sport in Thailand.

# Which animal would have the strongest bite?

**#36**

a. the African lion

b. the great white shark

c. the *T. rex*

## the *T. rex*

***T. REX* HAD THE STRONGEST KNOWN BITE FORCE OF ANY LAND ANIMAL THAT HAS EVER EXISTED,** chomping down with a force of more than 12,000 pounds (5,443 kg). **Scientists were able to conduct research on the bite force of *T. rex* by studying its fossils** and constructing 3-D models of the dinosaur's skull. They could tell from the shape of the *T. rex* skull that **its jaw muscles were extraordinarily large, even for an animal of its size.** Scientists also studied the bites of birds, which are a type of dinosaur, and crocodiles, the closest living cousins of extinct dinosaurs. Scientists used the digital models of the *T. rex* skulls to run experiments that imitated the dino biting down in similar ways to birds. From this simulation, scientists discovered that, **unlike birds, *T. rex* dinosaurs actually had a stiff lower jaw** that gave them the stability they needed to bite with such force.

### Instant Genius

*T. rex* dinosaurs had hollow bones, just like birds.

# The North Pole is made entirely of ice.

**#37**

RUSSIA

North Pole →

GREENLAND

CANADA

USA

ANSWER: **True**

**THE NORTH POLE ISN'T MADE OF ANY LAND; IT'S ALL ICE!** The ice that makes up the North Pole is **6 to 10 feet (1.8 to 3 m) thick and constantly shifting around,** making it very difficult to inhabit. Scientists have tried to set up labs there, but parking them permanently is tricky because of the ice's movement. Instead, scientists have developed "drift stations" that are able to move with the floating ice. **Because of climate change, the ice is melting at a faster rate each year,** endangering the animals that live in the area and decreasing the North Pole's size. **Because the North Pole does not have any land, there are very few land animals that make it their home.** Arctic foxes and polar bears sometimes wander into the area, but they don't stay for long.

**NOW YOU KNOW!**

To navigate the icy waters of the North Pole, you have to take a ship called an icebreaker, which has a strong steel bow made for breaking ice.

# What is
# nomophobia
## a fear of?

**#38**

**b.** being disconnected from your phone

**a.** hearing the answer no

**c.** missing out

**ANSWER: b**

## being disconnected from your phone

**NOMOPHOBIA IS THE FEAR OF BEING DISCONNECTED FROM YOUR PHONE.** This phobia usually stems from the need to be with other people. The symptoms of nomophobia are very close to those of anxiety, such as **shortness of breath, trembling, sweating, frustration, and disorientation.** Nomophobia is a newer phobia, coined in 2008 during a study about phone use in the United Kingdom. Technology provides help that we rely on, but it's also added pressure for many users. **Young adults are the most likely to be affected by nomophobia** because they are more likely to use their phones for social networking and feel pressure to do so.

**NOW YOU KNOW!**
Nearly 80 percent of Americans say they check their phones as soon as they wake up. The average person spends more than five hours a day on an electronic device.

**Instant Genius**
About 50 percent of people with **nomophobia** never turn off their phones.

**#39**

How
many
**moons**
does
**Uranus**
have? **a.** 0  **b.** 1  **c.** 27

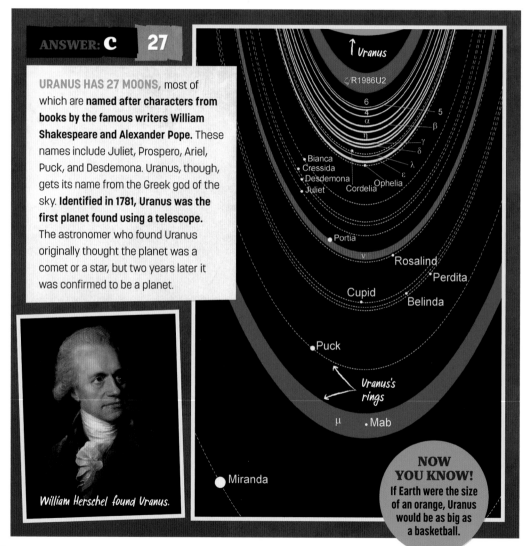

**URANUS HAS 27 MOONS,** most of which are **named after characters from books by the famous writers William Shakespeare and Alexander Pope.** These names include Juliet, Prospero, Ariel, Puck, and Desdemona. Uranus, though, gets its name from the Greek god of the sky. **Identified in 1781, Uranus was the first planet found using a telescope.** The astronomer who found Uranus originally thought the planet was a comet or a star, but two years later it was confirmed to be a planet.

↑ Uranus

ζ/R1986U2

6
4
α
η
β
γ
δ
5
λ
ε

• Bianca
• Cressida
• Desdemona
• Juliet
Cordelia
Ophelia

• Portia

ν
• Rosalind
• Perdita

Cupid
Belinda

• Puck

Uranus's rings

μ
• Mab

• Miranda

*William Herschel found Uranus.*

**NOW YOU KNOW!**
If Earth were the size of an orange, Uranus would be as big as a basketball.

**True or False:**

There are almost as many **bacteria** in your mouth as there are **people** in the world.

#40

Bacteria on the surface of a human tongue

ANSWER: **True**

THERE ARE 7.7 BILLION PEOPLE IN THE WORLD, AND MORE THAN 6 BILLION BACTERIA LIVE IN YOUR MOUTH. Whoa! But it's not as yucky as you might think. These billions of bacteria are broken into around 700 different species. **Some of them are healthy and good for your body,** but others are bad bacteria that can cause infections. The healthy bacteria protect your teeth from decay and cavities. **Luckily, only about 15 to 20 species of the bacteria in your mouth can cause infections.** These bacteria latch onto your teeth and gums and cause trouble. The good news: **Brushing and flossing your teeth can keep those bad bacteria in check!**

## Instant Genius

The average American spends 38.5 days brushing their teeth over a lifetime.

**#41** At what time does the Dalai Lama **wake up** every day to meditate?

a. 3:00 a.m.

b. 4:00 a.m.

c. 5:00 a.m.

ANSWER: **a**

**3:00 a.m.**

**THE DALAI LAMA IS THE BUDDHIST SPIRITUAL LEADER OF TIBET, A REGION IN CHINA.** Founded in India, Buddhism is a religion practiced in many Asian countries. **Buddhists believe that life is hard, and the goal is to achieve a state without suffering, which is called nirvana.** To do this, the Dalai Lama goes to bed at 7:00 p.m. and wakes up at 3:00 a.m. to meditate, read Buddhist texts, and write. **In the afternoons, he speaks to followers about Buddhism.** Born in 1935, he is the 14th Dalai Lama to ever lead. When he was only twov years old, he was chosen by the 13th Dalai Lama to take his place. Senior members of the Buddhist community had been led to the boy's house after seeing it in a vision. **Today, the Dalai Lama lives in India.**

The 14th Dalai Lama teaches students at his residence in India.

**Instant Genius**

The 14th Dalai Lama won the Nobel Peace Prize in 1989.

# Which animal can bite the fastest?

**a.** the vampire bat

**b.** the Dracula ant

**c.** the black cat

A Dracula ant puncturing the skin of a larva to drink its blood.

**ANSWER: b** **the Dracula ant**

THE DRACULA ANT CAN SNAP ITS TWO JAWBONES TOGETHER AT A SPEED OF OVER 200 MILES AN HOUR (322 KMH), making it the fastest animal movement ever recorded! Its jaws can go from a resting speed of 0 to 200 miles an hour in just 0.000015 seconds. **This is thanks to its unique flat shape of the jaws, also called mandibles.** The Dracula ant presses the tips of its mandibles together, which builds pressure. **Like the way we snap our fingers,** one mandible slides over the other for a quick release—then, snap! **Dracula ants use their super-speedy jaws to smack and stun their prey,** making it easier to capture and bring to their young for dinner. Dracula ants also use their jaws for defense, smacking their predators just like they do with their prey.

**Instant Genius**
There are more ants on Earth than stars in the galaxy.

# What creates the ocean's tides?

**a.** the moon

**b.** the sun and the moon

**c.** the equator

**ANSWER: b** **the sun and the moon**

**THE MOON REVOLVES AROUND EARTH, BUT ITS PATH IS NOT TOTALLY ROUND LIKE OUR PLANET**—it's more like the oval you'd see on a running track. **High tides, which is when water comes higher on the shore, happen when the moon is closer to Earth,** and its gravitational pull is stronger. Low tides happen when the moon is farther away from Earth and its gravitational pull is weaker. **There are two high tides and two low tides in a lunar day,** which lasts 24 hours and 50 minutes—that's how long the moon takes to fully rotate around Earth. The sun, which Earth revolves around, also plays a role. **When the sun, moon, and Earth are in alignment, solar tides move water toward and away from the sun**—but these tides are only half as large as lunar tides.

**Instant Genius**

The moon is about 240,000 miles (386,000,000 km) from Earth.

94

# When was **Halloween** first celebrated?

a. **50 years ago**

b. **200 years ago**

c. **2,000 years ago**

Rotten cabbage

**2,000 years ago**

**EARLY VERSIONS OF HALLOWEEN WERE CELEBRATED AS FAR BACK AS 2,000 YEARS AGO.** Halloween comes from many different Irish traditions. **One of the major ones is the Celtic festival for the dead called Samhain.** During this festival, the Celts believed that the dead came back as ghosts and roamed the world. **People would dress up in costumes** and leave offerings of delicious foods and corn dollies—handmade figurines constructed of corn husks—outside their houses to please the ghosts.

## Instant Genius

In some parts of Ireland, people celebrate Halloween with romantic games.

### NOW YOU KNOW!

In some American towns, Halloween was referred to as "cabbage night." That's because originally on Halloween night, or the night before, children would fling rotten cabbages against houses and prank one another.

A man and woman wear Halloween costumes at Bunratty Castle and Folk Park, County Clare, Ireland.

**True or False:** Lizards communicate by doing **push-ups.**

How many can you do?

#45

Western fence lizard

**ANSWER: True**

**LOTS OF LIZARDS DO PUSH-UPS WHEN OTHER LIZARDS ARE AROUND.** One reason? Lizards like to display and mark their territory. If another lizard is getting too close to their area, they will do push-ups to challenge that lizard to get off their turf. Doing push-ups helps them look larger and more intimidating. But a friendlier reason for a lizard to flex its muscles is to attract a mate. Male lizards will do push-ups in the presence of female lizards to both look larger and show off the bright colors on their bodies. **The male western fence lizard, for example, likes to flash his blue belly at other females.**

### Instant Genius

The European glass lizard has no legs.

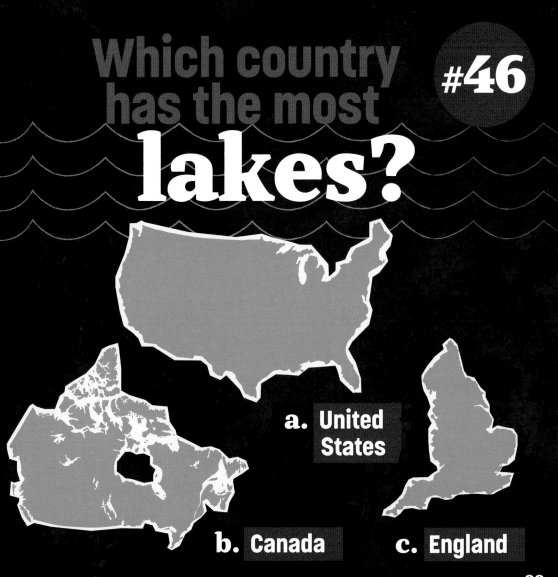

# Which country has the most lakes?

**#46**

a. United States

b. Canada

c. England

99

**THE GREATEST POPULATION OF LAKES IS IN CANADA.** There are about 1.42 million lakes around the world, and Canada is home to 62 percent of them. **That's 879,800 lakes!** Russia has the second largest number of lakes, with 201,200 lakes, and the United States is third, with roughly 102,500 lakes. **Lakes are most common in the upper parts of the Northern Hemisphere** because these areas were all covered with large sheets of ice during the last ice age. The sheets of ice created large craters in the ground. **When the ice melted, those depressions were filled with the remaining water.** Lakes can also form by the movement of Earth's crust, which creates basins that fill with rainwater or runoff.

**Instant Genius**

Canada's biggest lake is Lake Superior.

**NOW YOU KNOW!**

The world's deepest lake is Lake Baikal, in Russia. It is more than 1 mile (1.6 km) deep at its lowest point.

# Since 1880, how has the average global temperature changed?

**a.** It's increased.

**b.** It's decreased.

**c.** It's remained the same.

SINCE 1880, THE AVERAGE TEMPERATURE OF EARTH HAS RISEN 1.7 °F (0.94 °C). That may not sound like a lot, but even a small rise in temperature affects the planet in big ways. **Ice melts, which causes rising sea levels, flooding, and more extreme weather.** Human activities contribute to the warming climate, such as burning fossil fuels, releasing chemicals into the atmosphere, and cutting down trees. **When humans burn fossil fuels, like the gas we use in cars, the heat is absorbed into Earth's surface. This is what contributes to the global temperature rise.** These effects make life harder for both animals and humans. Scientists and lawmakers are working on ways to combat further changes to our climate, including reducing the amount of fossil fuels we use.

**Instant Genius**

More than a million species are at risk of extinction due to climate change.

Emperor penguin

The Hubbard Glacier in Alaska

# Fungi

## can be trained to eat used diapers and oil spills.

**#48**

103

Eat my shorts, fungi!

**ANSWER: True**

**BIOLOGISTS ARE BREAKING NEW GROUND WITH FUNGI,** a group of organisms that are unique from animals and plants. **Unlike animals, fungi can't move from place to place, and unlike plants, they can't make their own food.** Still, by preparing the right type of fungi and encouraging certain substances within them to develop, **scientists have discovered that fungi can do many things.** Fungi can be used to clean up some of the world's waste. **By pairing fungi with waste, the organisms can help break down and decompose not only natural waste but man-made waste as well.** Certain fungi even use enough pressure to break through Kevlar, which is a strong heat-resistant fiber.

## Instant Genius

Chemical compounds in mushrooms are being studied to help fight cancer.

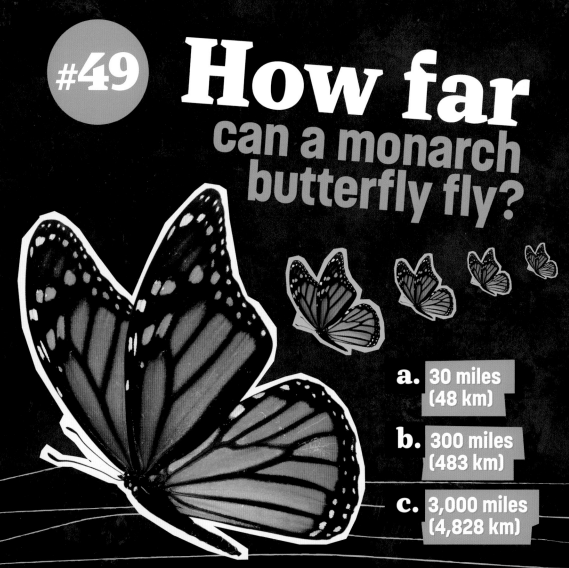

# #49

# How far
## can a monarch butterfly fly?

a. 30 miles (48 km)

b. 300 miles (483 km)

c. 3,000 miles (4,828 km)

**ANSWER: C**

# 3,000 miles (4,828 km)

UNLIKE SOME OTHER BUTTERFLIES, MONARCHS CANNOT SURVIVE IN COLD WEATHER, so they fly 2,000 to 3,000 miles (3,219 to 4,828 km) south for the winter. Monarch butterflies **start their journey in the fall from Canada and the northeast United States and travel as far south as central Mexico.** Once summer approaches and the weather warms up, **monarchs travel thousands of miles once again, back to where they started.** This generation, called the migratory generation, can live for up to eight months, while the summer generations survive just two to five weeks.

## Instant Genius

The milkweed that monarchs consume makes them toxic to predators wanting to eat them.

# What is the largest manned object ever sent to space?

a. **Hubble Space Telescope**

b. **International Space Station**

c. **Shuttle-Mir**

# International Space Station

**IN NOVEMBER 1969, THE FIRST SECTION OF THE INTERNATIONAL SPACE STATION WAS LAUNCHED INTO SPACE BY A RUSSIAN ROCKET.** Since then, it has been home to more than 242 scientists, engineers, and pilots. **The station is about the size of a football field and weighs more than 925,000 pounds (419,600 kg).** Today, it functions as a laboratory, where astronauts study samples taken from planets and asteroids, as well as the effects of space on the human body. **Since 2000, the station has been continuously occupied, usually by a crew of six people.** But the lack of gravity in space is hard on the body. To prevent muscle loss and bone decay, **astronauts must work out in the station's special gym for two hours a day,** where they clip onto certain machines so they won't float away.

## Instant Genius

In a single day, the space station can make 16 orbits around Earth.

### NOW YOU KNOW!

The International Space Station took 10 years and 30 space missions to build.

# 51

# What statement is not true about Nelson Mandela?

**a.** He was South Africa's first Black head of state.

**b.** He was the first South African leader to be elected with a democratic election.

**c.** He was born in Saudi Arabia.

Nelson Mandela at the age of 19

# He was born in Saudi Arabia.

**NELSON MANDELA WAS BORN AS ROLIHLAHLA MANDELA IN SOUTH AFRICA—NOT SAUDI ARABIA—IN 1918.** When he went off to school, his teacher gave him the first name Nelson. At the time, teachers in South Africa commonly gave kids names that were "easier" to pronounce. **As a university student, Mandela was passionate about activism,** which is an effort to make change in society. For many years, his country, South Africa, was a British colony. In 1961, it became a republic. **Even then, the country battled with racism,** which is when people are treated unfairly because of their skin color or background. **Mandela fought hard against apartheid, or the racial segregation of Black Africans,** working to end the racist rule that had been in place for a hundred years. **Though he served 27 years in prison for his activism, he was elected in 1994 to be South Africa's first Black leader,** in the country's first democratic election.

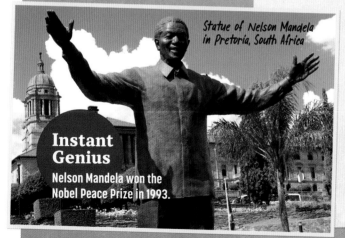

Statue of Nelson Mandela in Pretoria, South Africa

## Instant Genius

Nelson Mandela won the Nobel Peace Prize in 1993.

**True or False:** The DNA cells in your body could stretch to **Pluto and back.**

#52

ANSWER: **True**

IF THE DNA IN YOUR BODY WERE LINED UP END TO END, IT WOULD STRETCH 10 BILLION MILES (16 BILLION KM), enough to get to Pluto and back! DNA is found in the nucleus, or center, of cells, and it is very small. Why is there so much DNA in the human body? **DNA contains the instructions that tell our bodies how to grow, live, and reproduce.** These instructions must be translated into proteins for our bodies to understand them. **At any given moment, your body is decoding some of those DNA instructions** and building proteins. Now that's out of this world!

**Instant Genius**

All humans share 99.9 percent of the same DNA.

# What is the official sport of Maryland?

a. jousting

b. baseball

c. soccer

# jousting

A demonstration of jousting etiquette at Maryland's Renaissance Festival in Annapolis.

**JOUSTING IS A MEDIEVAL PRACTICE IN WHICH TWO RIDERS ON HORSEBACK CHARGE AT ONE ANOTHER WITH LONG WOODEN SPEARS CALLED LANCES.** Tracing its origins back to the Middle Ages, **jousting was first used to help train the cavalry**—soldiers who fought on horseback—for battles against their opponents. Soon jousting became a popular sport that was played by kings and other royalty. **Colonists brought jousting to the United States in the 17th century.** Much later, after the Civil War, there was a surge of interest in Maryland. **People in the state would dress in colorful costumes and reenact the medieval sport,** and in 1962 it became the state's official sport. It's still practiced today, but with a few changes. Instead of charging at another person, the rider charges toward a set of hoops, trying to stick their lance through one of the hoops.

## Instant Genius

In 1559, King Henry II of France died from injuries he got while jousting.

## NOW YOU KNOW!

The *Maryland Gazette,* the oldest continuously produced newspaper in the United States, began in 1727.

# Which cat is the biggest?

**a.** the Siberian tiger

**b.** the African lion

**c.** the snow leopard

**ANSWER: a** the Siberian tiger

**THE SIBERIAN TIGER IS THE BIGGEST CAT IN THE WORLD.** Generally weighing in at a whopping 400 to 660 pounds (181 to 299 kg) and **reaching more than 10 feet (3 m) from nose to tail,** this big cat trumps the African lion, which weighs between 260 and 420 pounds (118 to 191 kg) and reaches only 6.5 feet (2 m). Snow leopards are even smaller, weighing up to 120 pounds (54 kg) and measuring no more than 5 feet (1.5 m) long. **Siberian tigers have massive claws and powerful canine teeth.** To maintain their hefty weights, **these tigers can consume up to 60 pounds (27 kg) of prey in a single night,** though on average they usually eat less.

ANSWER: **True**

PLANTS ARE MASTER CHEMISTS, AND THEY USE THEIR ENERGY TO PRODUCE CHEMICAL WARNING SIGNS. There are many dangers for plants, including hungry insects, plant-eating fungi, and harmful soil conditions. When a plant is attacked by insects, **it wards them off by producing a chemical that is toxic to the insects or tastes terrible.** Another kind of chemical, called a volatile, warns other plants that danger is near. **Corn is a particularly good chemist and produces intense volatiles.** Corn's volatile smells like sweet flowers. It's triggered and released when a certain caterpillar gets its saliva on the plant. **When the flowery scent wafts over to other plants, the volatile prepares them for attack.** The rest of the corn cannot defend against damage, but it can prepare to heal faster.

**NOW YOU KNOW!**
Earth has more than 80,000 species of edible plants, including fruits, vegetables, and herbs.

# Whose hearts **beat faster:** men's or women's?

#56

a. men's hearts

b. women's hearts

c. It's a tie.

119

## women's hearts

THE AVERAGE MALE'S HEART BEATS 70 TO 72 BEATS PER MINUTE, WHEREAS THE AVERAGE FEMALE HEART BEATS BETWEEN 78 AND 82 BEATS PER MINUTE. Why do women's hearts beat faster? Women typically have smaller bodies than men, which means smaller hearts, too. **A smaller heart needs to beat more often to pump blood through the body.** Doctors are now realizing the importance of **understanding the differences between male and female heart function,** because problems like disease can appear very differently. With more information, **they'll be better able to treat these problems when they happen.**

Open-heart surgery

### Instant Genius
The average human heart is the size of a fist.

120

**#57** The famous painter **Frida Kahlo** was from what **country?**

a. Argentina

b. Mexico

c. Brazil

Frida Kahlo's studio in Mexico City

## Mexico

**FRIDA KAHLO WAS BORN IN COYOACÁN, MEXICO, ON JULY 6, 1907.** Her father was a photographer who inspired her love of art from an early age. When she was six years old, she contracted polio, a disease that crippled her right leg and caused pain that she carried throughout her life. **Then, when Kahlo was 18 years old, she was severely injured in a bus accident.** During her painful recovery, she started to paint self-portraits. She expressed her physical pain through her art. **Kahlo's style developed with her unique identity as a Mexican woman and an artist.** In the early 1930s, Kahlo traveled to the United States and came home with even greater pride for her Mexican culture. **She later became a professor of art at La Esmeralda, the national school of fine arts in Mexico City.**

### NOW YOU KNOW!
The 500 pesos bill in Mexico has the face of Frida Kahlo on one side and her artist husband, Diego Rivera, on the other.

### Instant Genius
Frida Kahlo did not become famous until decades after her death.

**#58**

# The United States and Russia are the only two countries in the space race.

Model of the European Space Agency's Ariane 5 space rocket at Guiana Space Centre in Kourou, French Guiana

**BOTH RUSSIA AND THE UNITED STATES HAVE BEEN LEADERS IN SPACE EXPLORATION FOR DECADES.** But now other countries, such as China and India, are joining in. **China successfully landed a rover on the moon in 2019 and has said it plans to return.** India had an unsuccessful voyage to the moon but plans to try again. And they're not the only ones. The United Arab Emirates teamed with Russia to launch a satellite orbiting Mars, and **the European Space Agency is planning a future moon landing.** Russia, part of what was formerly the Soviet Union, was the first to put a human in space. Americans, so far, have been the only ones to set foot on the moon. **But as technology advances, the solar system might need air traffic control!**

**NOW YOU KNOW!**
The first U.S. Apollo program to the moon in 1969 cost the equivalent of $260 billion in today's money.

APOLLO
NASA

# #59

**True or False:**

# A hamster's front teeth **never stop growing.**

125

**LIKE ALL RODENTS, HAMSTERS HAVE TWO FRONT TEETH ON BOTH THEIR UPPER AND LOWER JAWS CALLED INCISOR TEETH.** These teeth are different from human teeth because **they do not have roots and they never stop growing.** They are very strong and have the power to chew through plastic and several types of metal, including iron. **It's crucial that hamsters continuously file down their teeth to prevent them from becoming overgrown,** which can get in the way of a good chew. Hamsters have several methods of filing down their teeth. The first is by grinding their teeth together. **Hamsters also gnaw on wood and other objects to keep their teeth sharp and short.** In fact, the word *rodent* comes from the Latin word that means "to gnaw."

**Instant Genius**

There is a hamster species that can grow up to 12 inches (30 cm) long.

**NOW YOU KNOW!**

There are 26 species of wild hamsters that live in eastern Europe and central Asia.

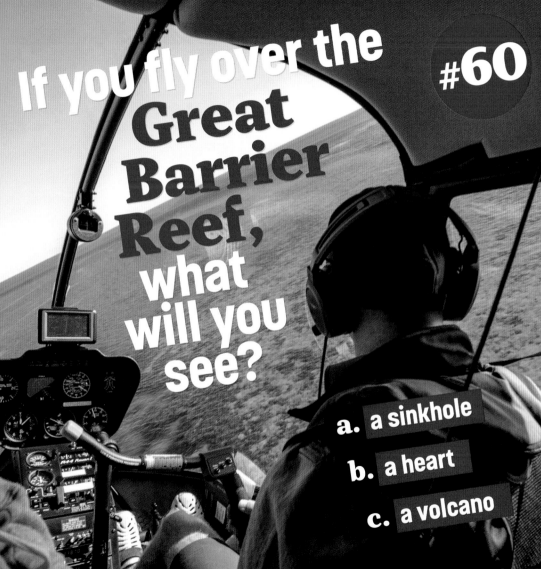

If you fly over the

# Great Barrier Reef,

what will you see?

a. a sinkhole

b. a heart

c. a volcano

The Heart Reef in the Great Barrier Reef, Australia

ANSWER: **b** **a heart**

**HEART REEF IS ONE OF THE MANY REEFS THAT MAKE UP THE GREAT BARRIER REEF ON THE NORTHEASTERN COAST OF AUSTRALIA.** One of the sseven wonders of the natural world, the Great Barrier Reef is filled with breathtaking beauty and awesome ocean life. **The 134,363 square miles (348,000 sq km) of the reef contain the largest collection of coral,** including 400 types, 1,500 species of fish, and 4,000 different types of mollusks. Within the Great Barrier Reef are 2,500 individual reefs, each with its own ecosystem. **The Heart Reef, named for its special shape, has become a big tourist attraction,** especially for couples declaring their love and even getting engaged. **The naturally formed heart shape measures less than 98 feet (30 m) wide.**

### Instant Genius

Around 10 percent of the world's fish species are found in the Great Barrier Reef.

**True or False:** Some blizzards can have **wind speeds** as strong as a hurricane.

#61

## ANSWER: False

THOUGH BLIZZARDS CAN HAVE VERY STRONG WINDS, THEY COULD NEVER RIVAL A HURRICANE. Blizzards are large snowstorms with winds blowing at least 35 miles an hour (56 kmh), and these storms can last for hours. **Hurricanes are similar to blizzards, but instead of snow, they carry rain.** And hurricanes can last for more than a week! **These massive storms have stronger winds than blizzards, starting at 74 miles an hour (119 kmh).** One of the worst blizzards in history, the 1913 "White Hurricane," had record-breaking winds of 60 miles an hour (97 kmh)—close to, but no competition for, a hurricane's minimum speed. For comparison, Hurricane Camille—a 1969 storm and **one of the most intense hurricanes to ever strike the U.S.—had wind speeds averaging 175 miles an hour (281 kmh).**

### Instant Genius
Hurricanes are classified into five categories based on their wind speed.

### NOW YOU KNOW!
About 40 percent of all hurricanes that touch down in the United States make landfall in Florida.

# How tall was the world's **tallest** dog?

you know, ruffly . . .

**a.** almost 5 feet (1.5 m) tall

**b.** almost 6 feet (1.8 m) tall

**c.** more than 7 feet (2.1 m) tall

## more than 7 feet (2.1 m) tall

**GREAT DANES ARE THE TALLEST DOGS IN THE WORLD.** They are also known to be very affectionate and social. **Freddy the Great Dane was the tallest of them all,** measuring 3 feet, 4 inches (1.01 m) when standing on all four legs, and a towering 7 feet, 5.5 inches (2.27 m) when standing on two legs. His owner, Claire Stoneman from Essex, England, loved him very much and **described him as "my happiness" and a "slobber bugger."** Freddy passed away in January 2021, five years after winning the world record for world's tallest dog. **Claire says that Freddy was actually the runt of his litter.**

**NOW YOU KNOW!**
Currently, Milly the Chihuahua is less than 4 inches (10 cm) tall, earning her the title of the world's smallest full-grown dog.

**Instant Genius**
Great Danes were originally bred to hunt wild boar.

**True or False:** Beavers live in **trees.**

#63

Beaver dam

Beaver lodge

**NOW YOU KNOW!**

Beavers make a sweet-smelling chemical was sometimes used in vanilla flavoring. They release the chemical, called castoreum, with their pee to mark their territory.

**ANSWER: False**

**YOU PROBABLY KNEW BEAVERS BUILD DAMS, BUT DID YOU KNOW THEY MAKE IMPRESSIVE HOUSES, TOO?** Beavers live in ponds, lakes, rivers, and other places near the water. Their homes, called lodges, are dome-shaped structures on lakes, rivers, or streams. **They're made by weaving together sticks, grasses, and moss.** Then the beavers spread mud around everything to hold it in place. **These lodges usually have several underwater entrances, so beavers can easily swim away from predators to safety.** Beavers can't breathe underwater, so the top sticks out above the water's surface, with a hole for air.

**Instant Genius**

Beavers can see underwater.

#64

True or False: There is an **active supervolcano under Yellowstone.**

ANSWER: **True**

A SUPERVOLCANO IS A VOLCANO THAT IS RANKED AS AN 8, WHICH IS THE HIGHEST RANKING ON THE VOLCANIC EXPLOSIVITY INDEX (VEI). To be a supervolcano, a volcano must release more than 240 cubic miles (1,000 cu km) of material during an explosion. That's more than twice the size of Lake Erie! **Yellowstone has produced three major eruptions, including two scoring 8 and a 7 on the VEI.** The most recent eruption was 640,000 years ago. But don't worry about another happening anytime soon. **Very few volcanoes qualify for supervolcano status.** Over the past 10,000 years, only 5,000 eruptions have been measured on the VEI, and none of them were classified as a supervolcano. In fact, **only 42 volcanoes have ever scored a 7 or 8 on the VEI in the past 36 million years!**

### Instant Genius

The magma under Yellowstone may exceed temperatures of 1475 °F (802 °C). That's almost twice as hot as the surface of Mercury in daytime.

**#65**

# How old would a two-year-old cat be if it were a person?

a. **2 years old**

b. **12 years old**

c. **25 years old**

## 25 years old

**A TWO-YEAR-OLD CAT IS EQUIVALENT TO A 25-YEAR-OLD HUMAN.** Because cats have a shorter life span than humans, a unique mathematical method was developed to measure how old a cat would be if it had the life span of a human. **Cats grow quickly and typically live for 16 to 20 human years,** whereas humans typically live for 85 to 90 years. **To compare the cat's life span to a human's, a different scale is needed,** so scientists came up with the following method: When a cat is anywhere from just born to a year old in human years, it's 15 years old in cat years. **Once the cat turns 2 years old, it becomes 25 years old in cat life.** After that, each human year is an additional 4 cat years. So, if your cat gets to be 21 in human years, it's 101 in cat years!

**#66**

**True or False:**

**No matter where you are on Earth, you always see the same side of the moon.**

ANSWER: **True**

**THE MOON ROTATES WHILE ORBITING EARTH.**
Meanwhile, Earth rotates around the sun. **The time
it takes for the moon to complete a full revolution
on its axis is the same amount of time it takes to
orbit Earth.** So, from Earth, we will consistently
see the same side of the moon. Though it may
seem complicated, imagine this: **You are Earth,
riding your bike in a circle.** Your parent, the moon,
is outside the circle, walking slowly around you as
you ride. **Every time you pass your parent, you'll
be seeing the same side of them.**

# Which has more muscles: a human or a caterpillar?

**a.** a human  **b.** a caterpillar  **c.** It's a tie.

A close-up of the Manduca rustica caterpillar eating a leaf

**ANSWER: b** a caterpillar

**THE HUMAN BODY HAS MORE THAN 650 MUSCLES.** Caterpillars, in comparison, have up to **4,000 muscles in their small bodies—with 248 muscles in their heads alone!** Caterpillars need all of these muscles to move and circulate blood through their long bodies. They move by squeezing their muscles in a wavelike sequence to propel themselves forward. This movement helps them escape predators and find food. **Caterpillars have six true legs to help them move too, plus several pairs of false legs,** called prolegs, along their bodies. These false legs have tiny hooks on the base that help the caterpillars cling to things. **Caterpillars also have very strong jaw muscles that allow them to chomp on many types of plants.**

## Instant Genius

Caterpillars increase their mass by 1,000 times over the course of their lives.

True or False:

# Dolphins hold their breath as they swim underwater.

#68

143

NOW YOU KNOW!
Dolphins hold their breath anywhere from 3 to 20 minutes when underwater.

Blowhole

ANSWER: **True**

DOLPHINS ARE MAMMALS AND NEED TO BREATHE OXYGEN, JUST LIKE HUMANS DO. This means when they go underwater, they have to hold their breath. **Unlike humans though, dolphins do not breathe out of their noses and mouths.** Instead, they breathe out of their blowholes, which are located on the top of their heads. **This spot makes it easy for dolphins to get air when their bodies reach the water's surface,** instead of lifting their whole heads out of the water. Dolphins can easily open and close their blowholes, keeping water from getting in their lungs when they're submerged underwater. Ever notice water spurting from a dolphin's blowhole when it comes up to breathe? **That water doesn't come from inside the dolphin—it's the water surrounding the blowhole that shoots out.**

## Instant Genius

There are around 90 species of cetaceans—a group including whales, dolphins, and porpoises.

144

# #69

## What can mild weather in the fall lead to?

**a.** more snow in winter

**b.** less homework

**c.** more spiders inside your house

145

## more spiders inside your house

**SPIDERS ARE FOUND ON EVERY CONTINENT EXCEPT ANTARCTICA.** Their diet mainly consists of mosquitoes, flies, moths, and sometimes even other spiders. When the winter comes with its freezing temperatures, most spiders die or go into hibernation. **But if there is mild weather in the fall, spiders get a longer season to munch.** The spiders that take advantage of the extended buffet actually increase in size by 0.1 inches (2.5 mm) making them heartier and healthier. **When the temperatures drop, these plump spiders take refuge by sneaking into your house,** where they will catch other bugs that may have crawled into your house looking for shelter, food, and warmth.

### Instant Genius

There are more than 45,000 known species of spiders.

**It's impossible to transplant a face.**

#70

Doctors in Barcelona, Spain, hold a press conference after their patient's face transplant surgery.

**ANSWER: False**

**THERE HAVE BEEN AT LEAST 45 PARTIAL AND FULL-FACE TRANSPLANTS DONE AROUND THE WORLD.** Like a heart or kidney transplant, a face transplant can be done for a person born with irregular features or seriously wounded. **The long and difficult operation takes anywhere from 16 to 30 hours.** When the transplant is done, patients typically gain or regain structure and movement in their face. **Then, the patient can better express themselves** and take part in activities most people probably take for granted, like eating, blinking, and smiling.

## Instant Genius

The first full-face transplant was performed in Spain in 2010.

## ✳71 Who was **Bluetooth** technology named after?

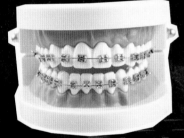

**a.** the inventor of dentistry

**b.** a 10th-century king of Denmark

**c.** an 18th-century artist

# a 10th-century king of Denmark

**KING HARALD OF DENMARK WAS GIVEN THE NICKNAME BLUETOOTH BECAUSE HE HAD A TOOTH THAT WAS RUMORED TO BE STAINED A BLUISH COLOR.** He ruled from around 958 to circa 985, **and is most well-known for uniting Scandinavia, a group of countries in northern Europe, by battling to bring together the tribes of Denmark.** How did a popular technology feature on our phones get named after a Danish king? **The technology's inventor was reading a book about Vikings at the time and decided to use it as a code name.** He thought it was fitting because, just as King Harald united the neighboring tribes, **Bluetooth connects neighboring devices.** Though many other names were considered, Bluetooth remained the name of the technology, **and the popular symbol is the initials of King Harald in the ancient letters, called runes, of** the Danish language.

**NOW YOU KNOW!**
In the time of the Vikings, skiing was both a way to get around and a recreational sport.

Which of these scenarios is the **deadliest?**

**#72**

b. **lightning strikes**

a. **shark attacks**

c. **bee stings**

**lightning strikes**

**SHARKS AND BEES ARE NOT AS DEADLY AS YOU MIGHT THINK.** Humans aren't part of a shark's normal diet, **so sharks don't usually go searching for humans when they're hungry.** Most attacks happen when a human accidentally bothers a shark first— or because the shark has confused the human for prey. **In the United States, there is an annual average of only about 62 deaths per year from hornet, wasp, and bee stings.** Lightning, however, is far more lethal. That's because the electric charge from lightning can stop your heart. **The chance of dying from a lightning strike is 1 in 500,000, compared with 1 in 3.7 million for a shark attack.**

**Instant Genius**

Certain species of sharks can shed 30,000 teeth in their lifetime.

**True or False:**

# Dogs can be ID'd with their noseprints.

**#73**

153

*The nose knows . . .*

**NOW YOU KNOW!**

Dogs can smell in 3-D. They smell with each nostril, and then their brain puts the scents together to make a picture of the combo.

**ANSWER: True**

**DOGS HAVE VERY UNIQUE *NOSE*PRINTS.** The way the ridges and bumps are formed on a dog's nose creates an identifying feature that veterinarians say is more reliable than any tag or collar. **The Canadian Kennel Club started to use noseprints as their main way to identify dogs back in 1938.** These days, many other kennels use it as well. **New apps are being created so that someone can use the pup's nose and their phone to identify a lost dog.** This technology is not yet widely used but has potential to be a quick and easy way to identify and return lost dogs.

**Instant Genius**

Dogs can smell time passing by noticing how odors change throughout the day.

# How many times can a **flea jump** without resting?

a. **300 times**

b. **30,000 times**

c. **3,000,000 times**

*Flea at 20x magnification*

**ANSWER: b**

## 30,000 times

**FLEAS CAN JUMP UP TO 30,000 TIMES WITHOUT RESTING AND CAN TRAVEL A DISTANCE AS FAR AS 150 TIMES THEIR OWN LENGTH!** There are more than 2,500 different species of these insects. At 0.13 inches (3.3 mm) on average, an adult flea is extremely tiny. **These bite-size bugs only live for two to three months, but they're mighty at spreading destruction.** Fleas are parasites, which means they feed on the blood of other animals such as dogs, birds, and sometimes even humans. **In the 1300s, these little critters hopped from person to person, spreading a deadly infection called the bubonic plague.** In fact, fleas have killed more people by spreading diseases than the total number of individuals killed in every war ever fought.

**NOW YOU KNOW!**

Fleas have backward-facing spines all over their bodies, making it difficult to pluck them from their hosts.

*Burying victims of the bubonic plague*

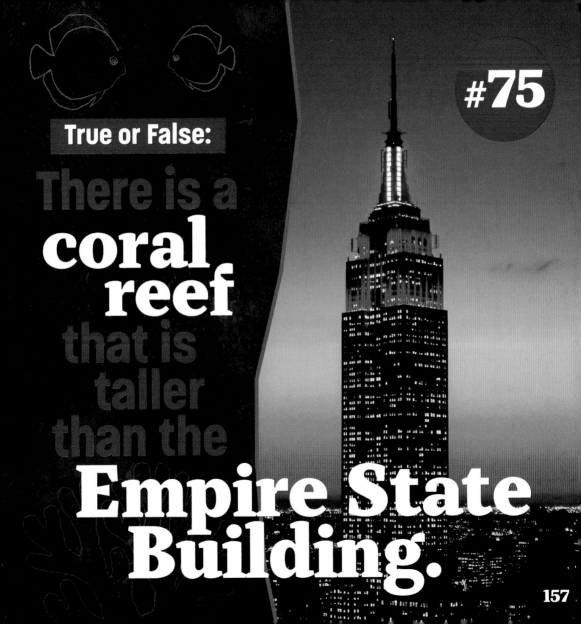

**True or False:**

There is a **coral reef** that is taller than the **Empire State Building.**

#75

157

SCIENTISTS WERE MAPPING THE GREAT BARRIER REEF OFF THE COAST OF AUSTRALIA when they discovered a new section of the reef that reaches more than 1,640 feet (500 m) tall below the ocean's surface. **That is almost 200 feet (61 m) taller than the Empire State Building!** Coral reefs are incredibly diverse, so it's no surprise that this new reef led to the discovery of up to 30 new species, including the longest recorded sea creature, a 148-foot (45 m) organism called a siphonophore. **Thanks to new technology, scientists can view detailed 3-D digital maps of the reef.** This discovery made it clear how unexplored the ocean is, and that there's many more reefs to uncover.

A reef seen from the International Space Station

**NOW YOU KNOW!**

The Great Barrier Reef is made up of nearly 3,000 individual coral reefs.

**Instant Genius**

Algae are what give coral its many colors.

How many separate **memories** can your brain hold in your **lifetime?**

#76

a. thousands
b. millions
c. billions

## billions

**YOUR BRAIN CAN HOLD BILLIONS OF MEMORIES THROUGHOUT YOUR LIFETIME.** However, different kinds of memory work in different ways. **Short-term memories are learned and forgotten quickly.** For example, going into the kitchen to get a drink, then forgetting to bring it with you. **Explicit long-term memories are things you try to remember,** like information for a test. **Implicit long-term memories, on the other hand, are remembered without trying,** and remembered more often—like tying your shoes. We're required to remember all kinds of information over the course of our lives, but don't worry about space running out in your noggin. **About a billion neurons in the brain combine in different ways to increase your memory's storage capacity.**

Neurons

### Instant Genius
Sleep helps you create memories.

*77

True or False:

# Snow is mostly trapped air.

*Inuit building an igloo in 1924*

**FRESHLY FALLEN SNOW IS ABOUT 90 TO 95 PERCENT TRAPPED AIR!** Why does this matter? The densely compacted air means that the snow is a great insulator. **Both animals and humans build caves and burrows into snowbanks because the dense air will trap the heat of whatever is living inside it.** Take chipmunks, for example. To prepare for hibernation, they dig small tunnels under the snow, where they stay cozy until springtime comes. Humans also have used snow to keep warm. **The Inuit, an Indigenous group in the Arctic region, built dome-shaped houses made of snow called igloos.** Using tools made of whalebone and metal, people carved these homes out of large blocks of snow. **Some igloos were big enough to shelter up to 20 people.** Today, most Inuit people live in permanent houses.

**True or False:** There's a song with a **frequency** only dogs can hear.

#78

ANSWER: **True**

IN THE BEATLES SONG "A DAY IN THE LIFE," A SINGLE NOTE AT THE END OF THE SONG REACHES A 20,000-HERTZ FREQUENCY, which is a tone only audible to dogs. The Beatles decided to add this note at the end of the song as a joke, **so when people played it, their dogs would react at the end.** Humans cannot generally hear anything above 20,000 hertz, but dogs can hear all the way up to 65,000 hertz. **Their great hearing allows them to detect changes in the environment, including potential danger.** Dogs can also change the position of their outer ears to zero in on specific sounds. When your dog lifts its ears or pulls them back, it's likely that your pup is tuning in to a specific sound.

# Which **basketball** player holds the current record for most points scored?

**a.** Kareem Abdul-Jabbar

**b.** Michael Jordan

**c.** LeBron James

## Kareem Abdul-Jabbar

**KAREEM ABDUL-JABBAR HOLDS THE NBA RECORD FOR MOST POINTS EVER SCORED IN A PROFESSIONAL BASKETBALLGAME.** Abdul-Jabbar played a total of 1,560 games in his career and scored an average of 24.6 points per game, **scoring 38,387 points in total.** He played for the Milwaukee Bucks from 1969 to 1975 and finished his time in the NBA with the Los Angeles Lakers in 1989. Though Abdul-Jabbar holds the record for most points scored in a career, **Michael Jordan holds the record for the highest average of points scored per game, with 30.1.** Michael Jordan played a total of 1,072 games in his career and scored a total of 32,392 points. Michael Jordan played for the Chicago Bulls for most of his career, ending with the Washington Wizards. **These two players are considered some of the best athletes of all time.**

### Instant Genius

Kareem Abdul-Jabbar is 7 feet, 2 inches (2.18 m) tall.

### NOW YOU KNOW!

Both Michael Jordan and Kareem Abdul-Jabbar received the Presidential Medal of Freedom in 2016 from President Barack Obama.

**#80**

Which mammal gives birth to **babies** the size of a **stick of butter?**

a. the tiger

b. the giant panda

c. the polar bear

ANSWER: b

## the giant panda

**THOUGH THEIR NAME MAY SUGGEST OTHERWISE, GIANT PANDA CUBS ARE USUALLY JUST 1/900 THE SIZE OF THEIR MOTHERS AT BIRTH.** Weighing in at just 4 ounces (113 g), they're about the size of a stick of butter. Only opossums and kangaroos have smaller babies in comparison. Why are baby pandas born so small? **They are in the womb for about 3 to 6 months,** but they only grow for about a month of that time, so they are born underdeveloped. Compare that to 9 to 10 months for human babies! **Scientists aren't sure why this happens.** Once they reach adulthood, giant pandas typically grow to be 4 to 6 feet (1 to 2 m) long when standing on two legs and **weigh 200 to 300 pounds (91 to 136 kg).**

### Instant Genius
There are fewer than 2,000 giant pandas left in the wild.

### NOW YOU KNOW!
Pandas mark their territory with urine, just like many other mammals, including dogs, cats, and monkeys.

**#81**

# Which month
## is the most common for
# birthdays
## in the United States?

**a.** January **b.** September **c.** November

## SEPTEMBER

| SU | MO | TU | WE | TH | FR | SA |
|----|----|----|----|----|----|----|
|    |    |    |    |    |    | 1  |
| 2  | 3  | 4  | 5  | 6  | 7  | 8  |
| 9  | 10 | 11 | 12 | 13 | 14 | 15 |
| 16 | 17 | 18 | 19 | 20 | 21 | 22 |
| 23 | 24 | 25 | 26 | 27 | 28 | 29 |

**ANSWER: b   September**

**THE MOST COMMON BIRTH MONTH IS SEPTEMBER.** In that month, **the most common days to be born are between September 9 and 20.** When it comes to naming a baby, whether born in September or another month, **the most common names have changed throughout the years.** For example, in the 1940s, the names James, Robert, Mary, and Linda were the most common baby names in the United States. **Between 2010 and 2020, the most popular baby names in the U.S. were Noah, Liam, Emma, and Olivia.**

### Instant Genius

September 9 is the most common birthday on the planet.

**True or False:**

Cats don't
**dream.**

#82

**CATS SLEEP AN AVERAGE OF 15 HOURS A DAY, WHICH GIVES THEM A LOT OF TIME TO DREAM.** Cats will sometimes twitch or move their paws while sleeping, which perhaps expresses what they are seeing in their dream. **Just like humans, cats have dreams about their daily lives.** The way you might have a dream about being in school or playing sports, **a cat might dream of hunting, playing with a toy, eating, or watching birds.** Because pet owners are a part of a cat's everyday life, **it's very possible that your cat dreams about you, too.**

**Instant Genius**

A group of cats is called a clowder.

**NOW YOU KNOW!**
Unlike humans, cats can usually smell when they are asleep.

**#83**

True or False:

# Toe prints
**are not unique.**

173

**ANSWER: False**

TOE PRINTS ARE VERY SIMILAR TO FINGERPRINTS, WHICH ARE UNIQUE TO EACH PERSON. The individual pattern of the print develops when a baby is still in their mother's womb. **The ridges on the toes and fingers develop based on how the baby moves within the womb** and the balance of chemicals within it. Though each print is unique, **there are three major types of prints: whorl, loop, and arch.** If you have a whorl print, your print is a series of circles, each getting larger than the next. The loop print looks like a rainbow shape, and the arch prints are a series of slightly curved lines.

**NOW YOU KNOW!**

The thickest skin on your body is on the palms of your hands and the soles of your feet. The thinnest skin is on your eyelids.

# How many species of dinosaurs have been discovered?

# #84

a. 70  b. 700  c. 7,000

A laboratory assistant carefully frees a fossil from rock.

**ANSWER: b** 700

**PALEONTOLOGISTS HAVE IDENTIFIED ROUGHLY 700 SPECIES OF DINOSAURS.** However, they believe that many more types remain undiscovered, and may never be discovered. **Paleontologists can determine ancient dinosaur species from their fossils,** which are the preserved remains or impressions of an organism from a past geological time. For fossilization to occur, an organism has to be covered with sediment—the stuff that settles to the bottom of a liquid, such as lava or sand—soon after its death. **Eventually, the sediment will take the shape of the organism and harden, making a fossil.** Unfortunately, this process happens very rarely. Still, paleontologists are hopeful that **there are more long-lost creatures waiting to be discovered.**

**Instant Genius**

The pigeon is a descendant of a group of dinosaurs that includes the fearsome *T. rex*.

**176**

#85

True or False: It's easy to **eat in space.**

ANSWER: **False**

**BECAUSE OF THE LACK OF GRAVITY IN SPACE, ASTRONAUTS HAVE TO TAKE PRECAUTIONS WHEN EATING AND DRINKING.** Liquids are always served in a pouch with a straw, so droplets don't float away, and food comes dehydrated in sealed bags. To cook it, astronauts have to squirt water into an opening in the bag, close it, and put it in a microwave. **A typical meal can take about 30 minutes to prepare.** The containers of food are attached to a tray with fasteners. The tray is then attached to the astronaut's lap or to the wall. **Meals may not be as tasty in space, however,** because the food's aroma, which stimulates appetite, quickly disappears in the lack of gravity.

**NOW YOU KNOW!**
In 1961, Yuri Gagarin became the first human to travel into space. He was from the Soviet Union, a large nation in Europe and Asia that broke apart in 1991.

**Instant Genius**
In December 2019, the first cookies were baked in space.

# smallest reptile
## is about the size of which object?

#86

**a.** a sunflower

**b.** a golf ball

**c.** a mouse

A male *Brookesia nana* on a fingertip

Actual size
0.85 inches (21.6 mm)

Forest in Madagascar

**ANSWER: a**

## a sunflower seed

**DISCOVERED IN 2012, THE *BROOKESIA NANA* CHAMELEON IS THE SMALLEST REPTILE ON EARTH.** The female is 1.14 inches (28.9 mm) long and the male is just 0.85 inches (21.6 mm) long. **Like most chameleons, it lives in Madagascar and wanders the forest floor.** At night, the very small creatures climb trees and take refuge under the leaves. This small subspecies belongs to a genus with at least 13 other small chameleon species. It has a projectile tongue, much like its fellow chameleons, which it shoots out to catch prey. **Because this reptile is so small, it feeds on mites and other tiny insects.** Scientists discovered only one male and one female, maybe because they're so small, or because many of the trees where they live have been cut down. **Thankfully, their habitat is now being protected, and scientists believe the species will survive.**

**#87**

True or False:

## Pluto is smaller than the United States.

The Moon

Earth

Pluto

Pluto, the moon, and Earth to scacle

**NOW YOU KNOW!**
If you weighed 100 pounds (45 kg) on Earth, you would weigh about 7 pounds (3 kg) on Pluto.

ANSWER: **True**

**PLUTO IS A DWARF PLANET.** This means it travels around the sun just like the other planets in our solar system, but it is much, much smaller. **At only 1,400 miles (2,253 km) wide, Pluto is half as big as the United States.** The dwarf planet is far out . . . literally—about 40 times farther from the sun than Earth is. It sits in the Kuiper Belt, which is a collection of small icy objects in orbit just beyond Neptune. **Pluto itself is an icy planet, with temperatures dipping far below those in Antarctica.** Pluto travels much more slowly around the sun than Earth does, taking 248 Earth years to complete one rotation. One day on Pluto is about 6.5 Earth days!

**Instant Genius**
The average temperature on Pluto is –400 °F (–240 °C).

**#88** How often does the **stomach lining** replace itself?

a. never

b. every five days

c. every five years

183

# every five days

**OUR BODIES ARE ALWAYS GROWING AND CHANGING.** To perform at peak, old cells are constantly dying and being replaced by new ones. **Different parts of the body regenerate or rebuild at different intervals,** depending on their job in the body. The cells in the stomach lining are replaced very often—every five days—**because we use lots of acids to help us break down the foods we eat.** Although these acids are helpful to use, they also cause harm to our cells. Growing a fresh stomach lining is very quick **compared to how long it takes a bone to completely replace all its old cells. That can take about 10 years!**

### Instant Genius

When you blush, your stomach lining also turns red.

*Stomach lining*

### NOW YOU KNOW!

Your stomach is about 12 inches (30 cm) long and 6 inches (15 cm) across.

**#89**

The composer **Ludwig van Beethoven** had which **disability?**

a. He was blind.

b. He was deaf.

c. He could not walk.

185

Portrait
of Beethoven
aged around 30

**LUDWIG VAN BEETHOVEN WAS DEAF.** Born in 1770 in Germany, Beethoven grew up to become one of the most famous classical composers in history. Though he demonstrated extraordinary talent as a child, **Beethoven started to have hearing difficulties when he was 28 years old.** By the time he was 44, the composer was completely deaf. Some historians believe that his disability was caused by a high amount of lead in his bloodstream, due to an ingredient that was popular in drinks at that time. **Other historians believe Beethoven's ears could have been affected by an autoimmune disease,** a condition that causes the body's immune system to attack healthy tissues. Though he lost the ability to hear, **he was still able to compose music by feeling the vibrations on the piano with his hands.**

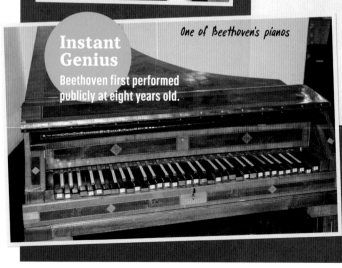

One of Beethoven's pianos

**Instant Genius**

Beethoven first performed publicly at eight years old.

**NOW YOU KNOW!**

An Arizona man bought 582 strands of Beethoven's hair for $7,000 in 1994.

**True or False:** Cats can drink **seawater.**

**#90**

187

**HUMANS SHOULDN'T DRINK SEAWATER BECAUSE OUR KIDNEYS CAN'T FILTER OUT THE SALT, BUT CATS DON'T HAVE THAT PROBLEM.**
You might think that drinking any kind of water would help you hydrate—but for humans, the extra salt in seawater actually pulls water out of the cells and causes dehydration. Cats, on the other hand, can drink seawater just fine. Of course, **even though cats can drink seawater, studies have shown they prefer fresh or filtered water.**

**Instant Genius**
Cats do not get as thirsty as dogs do. Cats once lived in the desert, so their bodies adapted to survive on less water.

**NOW YOU KNOW!**
When given the choice, cats prefer drinking moving water out of a fountain or a stream instead of still water in a bowl.

# How many seconds are in a day?

a. 860

b. 8,600

c. 86,400

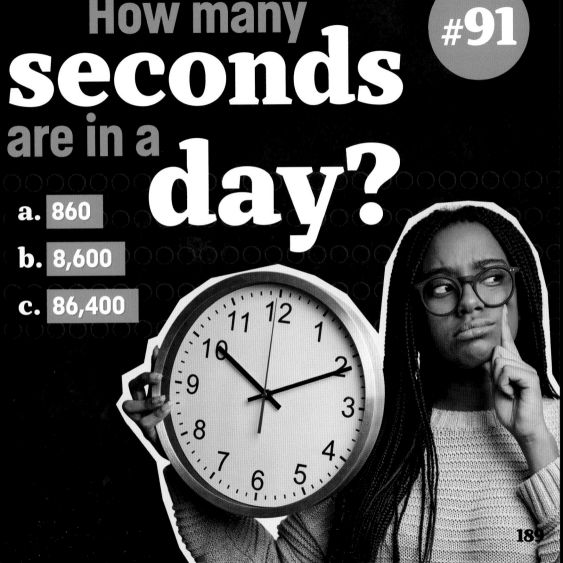

THERE ARE 24 HOURS IN A DAY, 60 MINUTES IN AN HOUR, AND 60 SECONDS IN A MINUTE. To find out how many seconds there are in a day, multiply 60 by 60 by 24 and the total is 86,400. **Do you ever wonder why there are 24 hours in a day, or 60 minutes in an hour? Well, thank the ancient Egyptians.** The Egyptians split days into 24 hours, 12 for daytime, 12 for nighttime. They used sundials, shadow clocks, and water clocks to tell the time. Egyptians chose the number 12 because they often used this number in counting. Instead of counting on 10 fingers like we often do today, **Egyptians would count on their 12 finger joints— three on each of the four fingers of a hand.**

**Instant Genius**

The average U.S. city commuter loses 38 hours a year because of traffic delays.

**#92**

What year did the **first** modern Olympic Games take place?

**a.** 1770   **b.** 1896   **c.** 1906

An illustration of Greek athlete Spyridon Louis winning the first Olympic marathon in 1896

**ANSWER: b**    **1896**

THE FIRST MODERN OLYMPIC GAMES TOOK PLACE IN
ATHENS, GREECE, IN APRIL 1896. There were about 280
athletes present—all men—**from 14 countries around the world.**
Hungary was the only country to send a national team. The
athletes competed in 43 different events in focuses such
as **track and field, cycling, swimming, gymnastics, weight
lifting, wrestling, fencing, shooting, and tennis.** The swimming
events were held in the Bay of Zea, off the coast in Athens.
Full of celebration, the Olympic Games were accompanied by
festivities and banquets. **An estimated 60,000 people attended
opening day of the 1896 Olympic Games.**

**NOW
YOU KNOW!**
Dimitrios Loundras is the
youngest Olympian to ever
compete in the Games. He
was 10 years old when
he competed in the
gymnastics event
in 1896.

**True or False:** It's impossible for a **fish** to walk on **land.**

#93

Mudskippers

ANSWER: **False**

**Instant Genius**

There is a type of catfish that can breathe air.

**SCIENTISTS HAVE DISCOVERED THATAT LEAST 11 SPECIES OF FISH CAN WALK ON LAND!** To learn how they walk, researchers studied the skeletons of the fish, focusing on their pelvic bones, spines, and ribs. The difference they saw: **The spines and pelvic bones of these fish are connected, giving them hips.** Hips are normal for land dwellers, including humans—but they're unusual for fish. **The walking fish also have four fins to help them move across land**—two in front and two in back, like salamanders. One of these fish, the cave angel fish, can walk on land *and* climb up walls!

**NOW YOU KNOW!**

The flying fish can glide through the air for distances up to 655 feet (200 m).

194

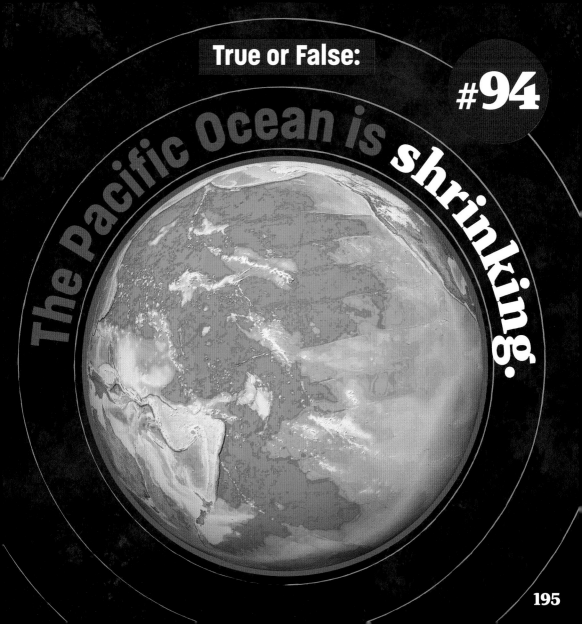

**True or False:**

The Pacific Ocean is shrinking.

#94

PACIFIC PLATE

Edges of plate

**ANSWER: True**

THE PACIFIC OCEAN IS THE WORLD'S LARGEST OCEAN, WITH AN AREA OF 63.8 MILLION SQUARE MILES (165.2 MILLION SQ KM). However, it's also shrinking at a rate of 0.19 square miles (0.5 sq km) per year. **The cause: activity with Earth's tectonic plates,** which are the large land pieces that make up Earth's outer layer. **These plates constantly push against one another, creating many of Earth's land formations,** such as mountains, volcanoes, and deep-sea trenches. When one plate is pushed under another, the process is called subduction. When the plates move away from each other, the ocean floor becomes larger, a process called seafloor spreading. **The Pacific Ocean is shrinking because the plates beneath it are moving closer together.**

### Instant Genius

The Atlantic Ocean is getting bigger as the Pacific Ocean is getting smaller.

**#95** Which group of **reptiles** has been around the **longest?**

a. turtles and tortoises

b. snakes

c. crocodiles and alligators

*Eunotosaurus africanus*

**ANSWER: a**

# turtles and tortoises

**TURTLES BELONG TO ONE OF THE OLDEST REPTILE GROUPS IN THE WORLD.** Paleontologists were able to determine from fossils that turtles date back more than 250 million years. ***Eunotosaurus africanus*, the earliest known turtle, lived roughly 260 million years ago!** These prehistoric turtles looked nothing like the ones we see today, however. **In fact, the earliest turtles didn't even have shells!** Over time, turtles have been able to change their physical traits in order to survive. The shells act as armor, protecting their fragile insides from hungry predators coming along to bite them. **The turtle's shell evolved over millions of years.**

**Instant Genius**
A turtle's shell is actually bone and grows with the rest of the turtle.

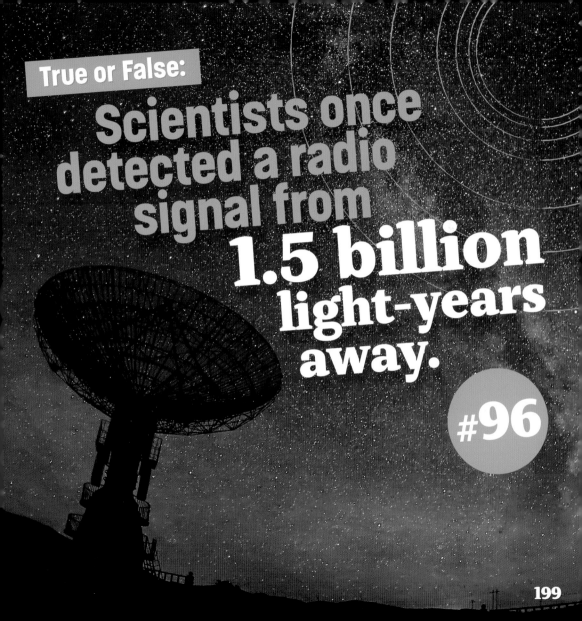

True or False:

Scientists once detected a radio signal from **1.5 billion** light-years away.

#96

CHIME radio telescope array, Dominion Radio
Astrophysical Observatory, British Columbia, Canada

**ANSWER: True**

ON APRIL 28, 2020, AT THE CANADIAN
HYDROGEN INTENSITY MAPPING
EXPERIMENT (CHIME) OBSERVATORY,
located in British Columbia, Canada, 13 fast
radio bursts were detected from 1.5 billion
light-years away. The observatory is home to
**four 328-foot (100-m)-long, superhigh-tech
antennas,** which are constantly scanning the
universe. In observatories like this all over the
world, scientists are getting fast radio bursts
that indicate something is happening out in
space. **There are many theories about what
causes fast radio bursts,** ranging from a rapidly
spinning star's strong magnetic field to alien
spaceships trying to connect with humans.
**So far, we still don't have a concrete answer.**

### Instant Genius

The Hubble Space Telescope is
the length of a large school bus.

**#97**

True or False:

# The clouded leopard

can't hang upside down.

**MOST BIG CATS ARE EXCELLENT CLIMBERS, BUT THE CLOUDED LEOPARD IS THE BEST.** This cunning cat lives in Southeast Asia, ranging from the Himalaya Mountains to lowland tropical rainforests. **Unlike most cats, clouded leopards can climb down trees headfirst, just like squirrels.** They have specialized paw pads, sharp claws, powerful leg and ankle muscles, and a long tail to help them balance. All these traits give the clouded leopard a grip strong enough to hang upside down from a tree. **This unique climbing ability makes clouded leopards exceptional hunters because they can ambush unsuspecting prey from above.**

**NOW YOU KNOW!**
Clouded leopards have been around the longest of any cat species. Genetic testing shows the cat is most closely related to big cats, such as lions and tigers.

**Instant Genius**
The clouded leopard is not in the same genus as leopards; it is its own.

# What do penguins sneeze out of their bodies?

**#98**

a. ice

b. salt

c. insects

**ANSWER: b** salt

**PENGUINS EAT A VARIETY OF MARINE ORGANISMS, WHICH THEY SWALLOW AS THEY SWIM IN THE OCEAN.** As they swim along, they also take in a lot of saltwater To get rid of all that extra salt, **penguins use a special organ called the supraorbital gland located behind their eyes.** The special organ removes the salt from their bloodstream. That filtered-out salt has to go somewhere, so what does the penguin do? It shoots the salt out of its nostrils! **Penguins can either shake their heads or, for a faster solution, sneeze to release it.**

**Instant Genius**

Some penguins mate for life.

**NOW YOU KNOW!**

Penguins have fewer taste buds than humans do, and they can only taste salty and sour things.

# Which planet has #99
## the most
# volcanoes?

**a.** Earth  **b.** Venus  **c.** Mars

**ANSWER: b** **Venus**

MAGELLAN MISSION TO VENUS

May 1989 to October 1994

**VENUS HAS MORE THAN 1,600 MAJOR VOLCANOES, AND MANY MORE SMALL VOLCANOES THAT HAVE YET TO BE COUNTED.** Because Venus is covered by a thick layer of clouds, scientists weren't able to get a good look at the planet's topography until the early 1990s, when the Magellan spacecraft used radar imaging to check it out. What they found surprised them. **Volcanic activity shaped much of the planet's landscape, with more than 90 percent of the planet's surface covered by lava flows and shield volcanoes.** Compared to Earth, these volcanoes are gigantic—nearly six times wider than Earth's largest volcanoes, which can be found on Hawaii. **Scientists do not know for sure, but they think some of the volcanoes are active on the planet.**

**NOW YOU KNOW!**

Venus has an air pressure more than 90 times that of Earth, the same pressure you would feel if you went a mile (1.6 km) down into the ocean.

**True or False:** **Robots** can be trained to think **independently.**

**#100**

**ROBOTS CANNOT BE TRAINED TO THINK INDEPENDENTLY, BUT THEY ARE ABLE TO LEARN NEW THINGS.** A robot arm created by Barrett Technology Inc., for example, was able to learn how to recognize a container amid other objects. Using that knowledge, the robot arm could retrieve and place things in the recognized containers. **Engineers have also been working on a "home exploring robotic butler,"** nicknamed HERB, that can complete tasks around the house or office. Using its two lasers and camera, HERB is able to navigate a kitchen, opening drawers and cabinets. HERB can also use programming to learn from human actions and imitate them. **Imagine if the engineers could get HERB to do homework!**

**NOW YOU KNOW!**

The word *robot* comes from the Czech word *robota*, which means "forced labor."

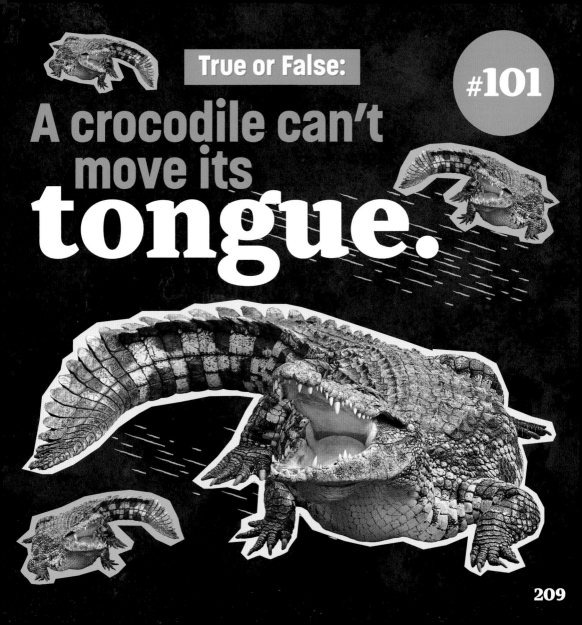

# A crocodile can't move its tongue.

**#101**

ANSWER: **True**

**A CROCODILE CANNOT MOVE ITS TONGUE.** Crocodiles have a special membrane on the bottom of their mouth that holds the tongue in place. **This is convenient, though, because if the crocodile wants to quickly chomp down, it doesn't have to worry about biting off its own tongue.** Crocodiles are carnivorous predators with very strong jaws and many sharp teeth. They catch both land and aquatic animals. For land animals, the crocodile waits in the water. **When an animal comes by, the croc launches a surprise attack, catching the prey with its powerful jaws and drowning it.** If the prey is bigger, the croc may tear it into smaller pieces first. Young crocodiles eat small fish, frogs, crustaceans, insects, and snails, whereas older crocodiles prefer larger fish and mammals.

## Instant Genius

Crocodiles can live in both saltwater and freshwater, whereas alligators live mostly in freshwater.

# Spot the 7 Random Differences:

Turn to page 215 for the answers!

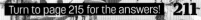

# Index

Page numbers in *italic* refer to images.

# Photo Credits

# Credits

Visit us on the Web! **rhcbooks.com**

Educators and librarians, for a variety of teaching tools, visit us
at **RHTeachersLibrarians.com**

Library of Congress Cataloging-in-Publication Data is available
upon request.

ISBN 978-0-593-51637-9 (trade)
ISBN 978-0-593-51638-6 (lib. bdg.)
ISBN 978-0-593-51639-3 (ebook)

COVER PHOTO CREDITS:
Front Cover Photo: Shutterstock.
Back Cover Photo: Dreamstime.

MANUFACTURED IN ITALY
10 9 8 7 6 5 4 3 2 1
First Edition

Produced by Fun Factory Press, LLC, in association with
Potomac Global Media, LLC.

The publisher would like to thank the following people for their
contributions to this book: Melina Gerosa Bellows, President,
Fun Factory Press, and Series Creator and Author; Priyanka
Lamichhane, Editor and Project Manager; Chad Tomlinson,
Art Director; Jane Sunderland, Copy Editor; Mary Stephanos,
Fact-checker; Potomac Global Media: Kevin Mulroy, Publisher;
Barbara Brownell Grogan, Editor in Chief; Thomas Keenes,
Designer; Susannah Jayes and Ellen Dupont, Picture Researchers;
Heather McElwain, Proofreader.